HOW TO HELP YOUR CHURCH GROW

HOW TO HELP YOUR CHURCH GROW

George E. Knowles

Review and Herald Publishing Association
Washington, D.C. 20012

Copyright © 1981
by the Review and Herald Publishing Association
Editor: Thomas A. Davis
Book Design: Kaaren Kinzer

ACKNOWLEDGMENTS

The quotation credited to Oscar C. Eliason is from the song "Got Any Rivers?" from *Favorites*, vol. 5, copyright 1945, renewal 1975, by Oscar C. Eliason. Assigned to Singspiration Inc. All rights reserved. Used by permission.

The quotation credited to Annie Johnson Flint is from the poem "Christ and You," copyright Evangelical Publishers, Toronto, Canada. Used by permission.

Library of Congress Cataloging in Publication Data
Knowles, George E., 1924-
   How to help your church grow.
    1. Evangelistic work. 2. Witness bearing (Christianity) 3. Christian life—Seventh-Day Adventist authors.
I. Title.
BV3790.K58   269'.2   81-5837
ISBN 0-8280-0082-4   AACR2

Printed in U.S.A.

DEDICATED

To Seventh-day Adventist laymen around the world who willingly give of themselves, their time, and their means to share Jesus and His message with others.

CONTENTS

PREFACE

This book is written for the laity of the Advent Movement, men and women who long to see the gospel commission completed so Jesus can return. It is written for those who have confidence that, under the power of the Holy Spirit, the assignment to share the good news with everyone can and will be completed—in our day, we would hope. It is written for lay persons who are concerned about deteriorating world conditions and who are motivated by their love for God and their fellow men to do something in Christian service.

The author believes that active involvement in ministries of service following conversion is the key to maintaining a close relationship with Jesus and to restoring His character in human lives. "When divine power is combined with human effort, the work will spread like fire in the stubble."—*Selected Messages*, book 1, p. 118. The divine power is available right now. Its release will be triggered by human effort motivated by love for Christ and lost humanity.

How to get started in personal evangelism and how to experience the close communion with Christ that will assure continuity of effort are vital questions. Therefore, while this book touches on the Why and the What, the emphasis is on the How.

God has great plans for His church in these momentous days. He has great plans for you personally as you catch a vision of the part you can play when you recognize His willingness to work through you.

Someone has said that the greatest tragedy is to reach the end of life and realize what God could have accomplished through you if you had only taken time to seek and to do His will for your life. In these pages may you catch a heavenly vision of service with Christ so that you will cry out as did Paul in the dust of the Damascus road, "Lord, what wilt thou have me to do?" (Acts 9:6).

HOW TO HELP YOUR CHURCH GROW

A CHURCH THAT'S MOVING

A little boy, alone with his father in the car, was unusually quiet until suddenly he cried out in great excitement, "Look, Daddy, I see a church moving!" Sure enough, a church building was being transported to a new location.

There is something exciting about a church that is moving, and there's something exciting about a movement that is nearing its destination. Both of these reasons for excitement exist in Adventism today.

How about your church? Is it moving? Is it growing? What is its rate of growth, and what are some of the things that could be done to help it grow faster?

When a church is moving it not only brings excitement, it stimulates research into the factors responsible for the growth. In this book we shall look at conditions that cause church membership figures to move upward. You will catch the inspiration of relatively simple things you can do to help your church grow.

Perhaps you're saying, "Now, look, I'm not a pastor. I'm not even a church officer. I'm just a layman. I want to see the church grow as badly as anyone does, but what can I do about it?"

Well, my friend, just remember that this book was written for you. Keep on reading. If your reading triggers some ideas and inspiration, then you can take another step. You can engage in a personal experiment in soul winning. Let me tell you about some other church members who did just that.

Follow-up

John and Ruth, both in their early 30s, are members of a growing suburban church with a membership of 150. A number of young couples have recently been baptized. John and Ruth have invited several of these new members for Sabbath dinner on different occasions. Conversation invariably included the question, "How did you first become interested in our church?" A pattern began to develop out of these answers that fascinated John and Ruth. The stories told by the new members revolved around friends, relatives, neighbors, and colleagues at work or at school. Others told of their first contact as being through Adventist literature or one of our radio or TV programs.

John was especially interested because he is the lay activities leader of his church. The lay activities council had been looking for a project to involve a greater percentage of the membership, some type of activity in which the new converts could also participate.

The council decided to encourage church members to make friendship visits with people whose names were in the interest file. In preparation they updated the file and added other names the members could supply, including neighbors, relatives, friends at work, and others who had shown some interest, as well as former members. This was the logical way to begin a visitation program, because these people had shown signs of interest.

At the door introductions varied to fit the background:
"We're representing the It Is Written telecast"; "You

14

requested study guides from Breath of Life, and we're here to deliver them''; "We're calling at the request of H. M. S. Richards, of the Voice of Prophecy''; "We're from the company you purchased the *Bible Story* books from,'' et cetera.

The visits were warm, friendly, and relaxed. People responded.

Those showing the highest interest were invited to a Saturday morning Bible class taught by a warm-hearted physician. (The pastor has two other churches to look after and can't be present at this church every week.)

People on the next level of interest were offered Encounter Bible reading guides or audio-visual studies. Others were listed for future friendship visits; still others were coded to receive notification of Five-Day Stop Smoking Plans, nutrition classes, socials, musical programs, or other activities in which they showed some interest.

Let me tell you what happened in the number one category—those invited to the Saturday morning Bible class. One month into the visitation program there were seven new adults attending the class. By the end of the second month there were fourteen. After three months there were twenty-one.

After the third month the rate of growth fell off somewhat. There was a logical reason: the members visited the best prospects first, so after three months they had contacted the most promising names in the interest file.* From this point growth came largely from new names coming in from regular seed-sowing sources and referrals from the enthusiastic people already attending.

After six months thirty interested adults were

---

* See Appendix, p. 159, for an example of what can happen when prospects from the interest file are neglected.

attending each Sabbath. Many of them were bringing their boys and girls to the children's divisions. Evangelistic meetings were held and fifty were baptized, including the thirty in the Saturday morning Bible class.

As John and Ruth watched the candidates coming up out of the baptismal waters one by one, John whispered, "Just think, all these jewels were buried in the interest file! What if we hadn't launched our friendship visitation program?"

Lay Bible Instructors

Clara Miller and Sue Jackson were middle-aged members of a rural church of about thirty members. You could stand on the front steps of the little church building and see only one house—the one where Sue, a recently reclaimed member, lived with her non-Adventist husband. The membership of the church was declining because families were moving from the country to the city.

Sue had regained her first love for Jesus and His message. Now she felt a compulsion to share this love with others. She wanted somehow to make up for the years of service she had wasted while out of the church.

In Clara Miller she found a kindred spirit. Clara had been dangerously ill; physicians had despaired of her life. But the members of the little church had prayed and God had performed a miracle of healing. In appreciation for God's goodness, Clara made up her mind to give herself to Him for service. She and Sue set aside one day a week to work for the Lord.

They began visiting the farm homes sparsely scattered throughout the surrounding countryside. In an age when most people say they're too busy for old-fashioned neighborly friendship, these visits were received with great appreciation.

The two women invested in clubs of missionary journals. As they became acquainted with the various families, they gave careful thought to their interests and left the magazine that seemed to be the most appropriate: *Message, These Times,* or *Signs of the Times.* The journals seemed to strengthen the developing friendships. The articles provoked questions and provided a basis for spiritual discussions. Monthly visits became regular because of the delivery of each new issue of the magazines.

After about a year Clara and Sue offered gift-Bible reading guides to their farm-family friends. Now they had a reason for weekly visits. This required more time, but the rewarding experiences they were having made them more than willing to devote extra time to their project. As interests deepened, they found opportunity to involve their pastor in the friendship circle. Invitations were given to the friends to attend the pastor's Bible class. In less than three years the two women were responsible for the baptism of seven persons—very good fruitage, we would agree, from the labors of two members in a small country church. Think of what the growth could be if even 50 percent of the members had such active soul-winning projects.

As we review the experience of Clara and Sue, we see four important steps.

1. Friendship
2. Literature
3. Bible studies
4. The pastor's Bible class

These soul-winning experiences began when two members decided to do something about their burden to reach the families in their community.

If you were to talk to Clara and Sue they would tell you that they felt very inadequate when they began. Neither of them had given Bible studies. But, you remember, that is not how they started out. They started by giving friendship. Then they gave a sequence of beautiful missionary magazines. By the time the need for Bible studies arose, two factors encouraged them that they could do it. First, the people were now their friends; they were not dealing with strangers. That fact alone took away much of the fear. Second, the gift-Bible lessons provided virtually a do-it-yourself method. To become acquainted with the material, Clara and Sue did the lessons themselves. Then they enthusiastically told their friends about the reading guides. "We're doing them, and if you would like to have them too, we could get together once a week and compare our answers," they suggested. They were not saying, "We'll come and teach you," but rather, "We'll learn together." This approach was not threatening to either our lay workers or their prospects. And best of all, it worked.

Hospitality Evangelism

Charles and Martha Morgan and their three children decided they would develop a soul-winning project around their gift of hospitality. Martha loved to cook, and the family enjoyed entertaining company in their home.

At least once a month Martha would provide for company when preparing Sabbath dinner. Their 250-member city church frequently had visitors. When there were no non-Adventist visitors the Morgans would invite a family in the church with whom they were not well acquainted. This by-product of the plan alone proved to be a tremendous blessing to the Morgans, as well as to their guests.

In many cases the Morgans' hospitality was responsible for a visitor returning to their church. This was true of Ron and Celia Thomas, who hadn't attended church since their marriage. Ron had an Adventist background, so when Celia expressed a desire to go to church, Ron agreed, provided it would be an Adventist church. The Morgans spotted the visitors and invited them home to dinner. This gesture of friendliness brought the young couple back the next Sabbath and the next, until they grew to be part of the church family. This newly established relationship was made official in a beautiful service of baptism, with Charles and Martha Morgan standing as the Thomases' spiritual guardians.

Ron and Celia Thomas were by no means the only fruitage of the Morgans' hospitality evangelism. In the city where they lived was a technical college at which a small number of Adventist students from other parts of the State were enrolled. The Morgans opened their home on Sabbath afternoons to these out-of-town students. But they did more. They encouraged the Adventist young people to bring their non-Adventist friends for refreshments and social activities on Saturday nights. These contacts often led to Sabbath dinner invitations, coupled with attendance at Sabbath school and church. Each year there would be two or three baptisms resulting from the Morgans' hospitality evangelism.

The gift of hospitality can be cultivated in many Adventist homes. It is a form of soul winning in which every member of the family can participate. One couple I know has been very successful in winning neighbors through hospitality. Even when their children were small one of them was called upon to offer the blessing when non-Adventist guests were present at the table.

"Thank You for these new friends in our home. Thank You for the food we have, and may hungry people everywhere have food also, we pray in Jesus' name. Amen." Such would be the child's prayer. Hearts were touched, and more than one credited the chil-

19

dren's prayers as the influence that awakened their interest.

Natural and appropriate subjects for conversation when guests are in your home include family, occupation, and religion. And often there will be opportunity to share your testimony of God's goodness and grace.

Hattie Johnson was a widow. For some time after the death of her husband she dreaded going to church to sit alone. Then she developed her own hospitality project. Hattie would go to church early, sit near the back, and watch for a lady visitor sitting all alone. Then she would move forward, sit beside the visitor, and offer a friendly smile and a warm handshake. After the service, in the foyer or outside the church nonverbal communication would give way to verbal. Often Hattie would invite her new acquaintance home for lunch. Beautiful friendships developed, and Hattie's ministry eased her loneliness and that of many others, as well. Not only that; more than one person says, "I'm a member of the family of God today because of Hattie's hospitality."

And then there is the physician and his wife who reserve one evening each week for a fellowship dinner in their home. They invite patients, neighbors, Five-Day Plan contacts, et cetera. Dinner is followed by an informal, unstructured Bible discussion on whatever themes are of most interest to the majority present. Several baptisms result each year.

Perhaps you will want to consider some form of hospitality evangelism as a possible project for you or your family.

Tactics for the Timid

Matilda Maxwell was a quiet, unassuming Adventist housewife and mother whose small children required her to stay close to home. The Maxwells live in a neighborhood where there were many young couples with children about the age of their own. Sewing was one of Matilda's talents. She made virtually all her children's clothes. As the children proudly told their playmates that their mother made their clothes, Matilda became the object of admiration on the part of many of the other mothers who did not possess sewing skill.

Matilda offered to share her sewing know-how, and several of the women and older girls in the community accepted the offer. Friendships developed around the sewing machine. Questions about a tune Matilda might be humming, or some objects she was preparing for her primary class at Sabbath school, made it easy for her to invite mothers to bring their little ones to Sabbath school, "just for a visit." That first visit was usually the kind that made them want to come back for more.

Matilda's willingness to share won the confidence of her neighbors, many of whom turned to her with their problems and perplexities in areas other than sewing.

If you asked Matilda Maxwell if she had ever given a Bible study she would probably say No. And perhaps she has not given a formal study, although her Bible answers to neighbors' questions have served the same purpose. In spite of her natural timidity she found she could pray with her neighbors about their problems once they became acquainted. In her first two years of sewing-machine evangelism Matilda was responsible for three baptisms.

Audio-Visuals

Joe Lindell invested in a Dukane projector. So pleased was he with his purchase that he took it to work with him to show the boys. Joe was a square-shouldered, muscular man who worked in a warehouse. During a lunch break he proudly displayed his new machine, which looked like a portable television set and combined the features of a projector and cassette recorder.

"I've got 20 films about the Bible," Joe explained. "Some of them explain the prophecies of Revelation and have a lot to do with what's happening in the world right now. If any of you would like to have me bring the machine over so you and your wife and family can see these pictures, just let me know."

In no time Joe's enthusiastic offer resulted in his being booked up five nights a week for Bible studies— though he did not call them that initially. He just talked about showing films featuring the prophecies. Several of the families were so pleased they invited neighbors in to share the treat. One family asked if they could invite their pastor. The Protestant pastor was so pleased with what he saw that he invited the Adventist warehouse man to take over the Sunday evening meetings in his church for twenty weeks. The result? Baptisms, including that of the non-Adventist pastor and his wife. Joe's machine gave the information, but Joe was willing to give of his time with a warm and friendly spirit.

Admittedly, every soul-winning attempt does not result in a baptism. Even Jesus Himself did not succeed in winning all the people He contacted. So we must learn the lesson of perseverance. We must also strive to develop the ability to discern genuine interest. There are some valuable things we can learn about receptivity and indicators of interest. These things will be discussed later in this book.

The reading of the remaining pages of this book will trigger some, perhaps all, of these responses:

1. You will think about a personal or family soul-winning project.

2. You will catch an inspiration of what that project might be—something in harmony with your gifts and talents.

3. You will experience feelings of inadequacy.

4. You will feel the need of drawing closer to the Lord.

Sometimes the inspiration gained from reading a book or attending a lay congress or seminar heightens a burden to see every one of your fellow church members working for souls. What can one individual do in such a situation? Perhaps the answer is found in this inspired statement: "When churches are revived, it is because some individual seeks earnestly for the blessing of God. He hungers and thirsts after God, and asks in faith, and receives accordingly. He goes to work in earnest, feeling his great dependence upon the Lord, and souls are aroused to seek for a like blessing, and a season of refreshing falls on the hearts of men. The extensive work will not be neglected. The larger plans will be laid at the right time; but personal, individual effort and interest for your friends and neighbors, will accomplish much more than can be estimated."—*Christian Service*, p. 121.

Let us take a closer look at what we've just read: One person who earnestly seeks for the blessing of God can bring revival to a church. He must act in faith. He must go to work for God, not waiting for others to join him. He must feel his great dependence upon the Lord.

The result: other souls will be aroused to seek for a like experience. Larger plans will be laid involving more of the members when they are ready to participate. All this will begin when one soul who hungers and thirsts to see a church moving makes personal, individual efforts for friends and neighbors.

> PRINCIPLE: *Revival can begin with one sincere person.*

Suggestions for Discussion

1 What can you do to help your church follow up the names in the interest file?

2 Clara and Sue evidently didn't have a job outside the home. Would their project have been realistic if they both worked five days a week?

3 What projects might be practical for wives who are employed full time outside the home? Think of some projects for men.

4 Discuss the circumstances that motivated Clara and Sue to team up in personal evangelism. Do you feel a lack of motivation personally? If so, what could you do to remedy the situation? What might others do?

5 Do you like the idea of comparing answers with your prospect once a week, or do you prefer the teacher-pupil relationship?

6 Does your church have an adequate hospitality plan? Does every visitor receive a dinner invitation? When did you last invite a visitor to your home for Sabbath dinner?

7 What possibilities do you see in working for people in your area who are away from their homes, such as the students at the technical college referred to in this chapter?

8 What talents do you have that could be used to make friends, as Matilda did with her sewing?

9 Discuss the advantages and disadvantages of audio-visual Bible studies.

10 What is your personal response to chapter 1?

GIFTS, GROUPS, AND GROWTH

Three key words you will encounter in this chapter are *gifts, groups,* and *growth.* First, let's give some thought to the fascinating subject of growth. Many a home has marks on the walls of the children's bedrooms indicating growth in stature between birthdays, or some other intervals. Human growth results from the growth and division of the body cells. These cells are programmed so that when they reach a certain size they divide in two. From this principle of cell division in the natural world we can learn a valuable lesson of spiritual growth: A unit subdivided into smaller entities will grow more rapidly than a single unit with no subdivisions. In the physical world it is a case of divide or die. Where there is no growth there will surely be death.

Church Growth

Let's look at the church in Pleasantville. Five years ago the local elder helped this church to become conscious of growth, or the lack of it. A business executive, he applied some management principles to the work of the church. The membership at that time was sixty. Over the preceding five years there had been ten additions to membership by baptism or profession of faith. With this information in hand the church board now had the answer to the first of three important questions related to growth. The question: Where have we come from?

There was no consistent pattern to the growth of the Pleasantville church. It was up one year and down the next.

The second question to which the church board addressed itself was, Where are we going? It decided that a consistent pattern of growth would be possible under the blessing of the Lord and with the cooperation of the church members. The board was careful to make its objectives attainable but at the same time challenging.

Its research* revealed that for the past five years the church had been growing at an average accession rate of about 4 percent per year.

Setting Goals

After careful study the board voted to aim at a 6 percent accession rate for the first year in a five-year projection, and to increase this by 1 percent each year so that by the fifth year they would reach a 10 percent accession rate.

The next step was to study the matter of how they would reach these objectives. On a blackboard they began listing suggestions, which included the following:

1. Take a deep spiritual interest in the youth of the church to create a climate conducive to decision for Christ and church membership. Many subdivisions were listed under this, such as striving to have all the children of Adventist families in Adventist schools,

---

* See Appendix, p. 159, for work sheets and methods used by the Pleasantville church.

Sabbath school classes for the young people that emphasize and lead to the conversion experience, opportunities for soul-winning involvement, and a wholesome social program.

2. Be sure that all visitors to the church receive a warm welcome, including an invitation for Sabbath dinner in an Adventist home or at a fellowship dinner at the church.

3. Increase the number of Bible studies given and improve the quality of Bible studies through a training program.

4. Encourage every church member to enlarge his circle of non-Adventist friends with a view to influencing them in favor of Christ and His teachings.

5. Pursue ways and means of drawing relatives and neighbors of Adventist church members into the fellowship circles of the church.

6. Follow plans to increase the number of non-Adventist visitors attending the services of the church.

7. Plan for consistent, intelligent, and loving follow-up of all known interests, including paid-out Home Health Education Service accounts, media and missionary journal names, Community Services clients, and all other names in the interest file.

8. Increase the number of enrollees in Bible correspondence courses.

9. Increase the volume of literature distributed.

10. Encourage consistent cultivating of family territories.

11. Help members discover and exercise their spiritual gifts.

12. Employ the principle of subdividing into smaller groups, making each group (such as Sabbath school classes) growth conscious.

A chart was made listing goals for measurable activities.

Weekly Objectives*

	Per Member	Per Class/Band
Bible studies given		
Pieces of literature given		
Bible course enrollments secured		
Non-SDAs brought to services		
Hours spent witnessing		
Gospel presentations given		
(Add to the list)		

The Pleasantville church wisely recognized the need for monitoring progress. This became the number one priority at each monthly church board meeting. Once a quarter the church had a special fellowship dinner, with time devoted in the afternoon for a sharing of progress and plans. A new sense of mission gripped the members. Optimism and enthusiasm were the order of the day. Everything in the church began to grow. During the first year of their new emphasis, the church achieved not a 6 percent accession rate but a 10 percent rate. The members decided to revise their projection, adhering to the objective of a 1 percent increase in accession rate each year above the previous year. Their fifth year showed a 16 percent annual accession rate—2 percent above the revised projection. New members caught the spirit of growth and were among the most productive as they reached out in their circles of influence to win friends and relatives.

Every group within your church should have a plan for growth and for winning new members. This should be true of the choir, the Dorcas Society, the Adventist youth organization, the children's divisions of the

---

* To guide in setting these objectives you might want to make a similar chart based on present accomplishments.

Sabbath school, as well as the adult divisions, the church school, and any other church-sponsored organization.

Remember the three important questions that need to be asked: Where have we come from? Where are we going? How do we get there?

Statement of Mission

Most Seventh-day Adventists are able to give a fairly clear statement of the gospel commission. It is not too difficult to define what the Lord requires of the church collectively. However, a statement of mission for your local congregation, or for your household, as an Adventist family and a subdivision of the congregation, is a somewhat more difficult matter.

Few of us will be called upon to go to other parts of the world to preach the gospel. None of us will be able individually to preach to every creature. So how do we relate our individual mission and the mission of the church to the total commission as given by Jesus to the entire church? Many congregations are finding it worthwhile to formulate a statement of mission, setting forth the reason for their existence as a church. Often the pastor asks the local elder to guide the congregation in developing a statement of mission.

One congregation—we'll call it the Homedale church—came up with the following statement of mission: "The Homedale Seventh-day Adventist church conceives of its mission as touching the lives of its members with redemptive action, teaching them to live in today's complex society as Jesus lived, and developing this saving relationship by growing in grace and by witnessing to others, and sharing the everlasting gospel with all those within the territory of the church."

By their response to a pastoral letter regarding the

statement of mission and by attendance at a church business meeting to consider the statement every member of the congregation had a voice in shaping it. Many members testified to the benefits derived from having their thoughts concentrated on this subject. Objectives were set for growth in harmony with the statement of mission.

Sabbath School Class Units

Instruction was given to the Sabbath school teachers on how to lead a group to set goals. Each Sabbath school class agreed on specific soul-winning objectives and activities they would engage in. With some minor adjustments the aggregate of the goals set by the individual Sabbath school classes became the objectives for the church.

The same groups that set the objectives decided on ways and means to reach them. Strategies decided upon included the following:

1. Deepen the personal commitment to Christ of individual church members.

2. Create among the members a new awareness of the relevance of the doctrinal position of Seventh-day Adventists to the needs of the community.

3. Make the weekly worship service reverent, friendly, spiritually satisfying, and heartwarming for every age group.

4. Attempt to meet the basic Christian social needs of each age group.

5. Keep the value of a human soul in the light of Jesus' sacrifice ever before the members of the congregation.

6. Aid individual members in discovering, understanding, developing, and employing their God-given gifts and talents in soul-winning service.

The Homedale church adopted as a motto, "Love in Action." It was thrilling to watch the transformation in this church as the motto influenced the lives of the members and the church came to reflect it.

Small Groups

Because of the emphasis on spiritual gifts, it seemed natural to encourage the development of small groups or bands, each made up of individuals with similar gifts and interests, and dedicated to a different type of soul-winning service. The Homedale church, with a membership of 500, had 44 active groups, including:

1. Ministry for the blind, part of which was reading and writing letters, et cetera.
2. Instruction in nutrition and healthful cooking.
3. The Five-Day Plan to Stop Smoking.
4. Personal witnessing.
5. Audio-visual Bible studies.
6. It Is Written follow-up.
7. General media follow-up.
8. Bible correspondence course enrollment.
9. Cassette ministry for shut-ins.
10. Cassette ministry for non-Adventists.
11. Ministry to the material and spiritual needs of the poor.

In the success of the small-group ministry outreach at the Homedale church we can hear echoed the words, "The formation of small companies as a basis of Christian effort has been presented to me by One who cannot err."—*Christian Service*, p. 72.

> *PRINCIPLE: The formation of small companies for soul winning is in accordance with the divine plan.*

There is a dynamic force in small groups made up of people who share common interests and objectives. Within the group there can be the sharing of problems and solutions, joys and frustrations, plans and results. There is great prayer and fellowship potential in such groups. There is also great service potential. The four men who carried the cot and brought the palsy patient to Jesus is an example (see Mark 2:1-5).

Spiritual Gifts

There are three passages in the Bible that deal specifically with talents and spiritual gifts: Matthew 25:13-30; 1 Corinthians 12:4-11; Ephesians 4:8-12; Romans 12:6-8. The chapter entitled "Talents" in *Christ's Object Lessons* (beginning on page 325) has very helpful material on this subject. It is possible that your pastor, or someone from the conference office, could conduct a talents-and-spiritual-gifts seminar for your church. Until help becomes available you can begin your own discovery of your spiritual gifts on a simple do-it-yourself basis. Here is a suggested procedure to follow:

1. Pray that God will guide you in discovering your spiritual gifts.

2. Renew your commitment to dedicate your gifts to Christ's honor and service.

3. Make a list of all the spiritual gifts you can think of. Use the three Bible passages mentioned and the chapter on talents in *Christ's Object Lessons* to stimulate your thinking.

4. When your list is completed, underline the gifts you believe you possess.

5. Arrange your gifts in order of priority, so that number one will be what you feel is your strongest.

6. Discuss spiritual gifts with other individual

33

Christians, or in small groups, and ask for the opinion of others as to what gifts you possess.

7. Compare your opinion with that of others regarding your gifts.

8. Exercise your gifts and you will discover they grow with use.

9. Remember that all gifts are for the ultimate purpose of winning souls.

10. Test your experience by the following questions. Does the exercise of my gifts result in:

    a. A closer walk with God?
    b. Harmony with church organization?
    c. Unity with fellow church members?
    d. Contention and strife?
    e. Pride and glorification of self?

11. Does your understanding of spiritual gifts make you a more devoted witness for Christ, or does it give you an excuse to avoid active service?

The experiences of the members of the two churches referred to in this chapter remind us that as many members as possible should participate in establishing the goals. When more members are involved in setting the objectives, more will be willing to participate in reaching them. Dividing large groups into small units will result in greater participation. This underscores the value of forming small companies within the church for service.

Spiritual Gifts

1. Which of the following gifts do you feel you have?
    1. Hospitality
    2. Comfort
    3. Language (if you know a second language)
    4. Helps
    5. Teaching

2. List other gifts you may have:
    1.
    2.
    3.

3. List ways your gifts might be used to win souls:
    1.
    2.
    3.

4. List three activities you could engage in within your neighborhood and/or territory in harmony with your gifts:
    1.
    2.
    3.

Suggestions for Discussion

1 List the units within your church that could be expected to grow through the process of "cell division."

2 Discuss management principles that can be applied to church growth.

3 In measuring church growth, discuss the matter of net membership growth (gain or loss in membership from all sources) in relation to gain by baptism and profession of faith only.

4 Discuss the list of 12 suggestions for church growth in relation to your church. Add to the list of suggestions.

5 Surveys show that new members are most productive in soul winning during their first three years in the church. Discuss possible reasons for this.

6 If all the members have a part in formulating a statement of mission and specific objectives for growth, what effect do you think it would have on their faithfulness in reporting missionary activity?

7 Is it possible to monitor progress accurately without a system of reporting?

8 Discuss the discovery and exercise of spiritual gifts.

9 How have you used your spiritual gifts since you were baptized?

SPECIALIZING IN THE IMPOSSIBLE

God brought the Israelites to the banks of the Jordan River in the spring of the year. The melting snows from the mountains had brought the river to flood stage, making it impossible to cross at the usual fording places. Only a miracle from God would make the crossing possible.

Notice three points in the experience of ancient Israel at the Jordan.

1. God's challenge.
2. The response of God's people.
3. The necessity of spiritual preparation.

In Joshua 1:2, we find God's challenge to His people, "Arise, go over this Jordan." Their response can be summarized in two words: "They removed" (chap. 3:1). God gave the assignment and His people moved.

It is significant that as they began to move forward they reached a point in their experience when they were receptive to the admonition "Sanctify yourselves: for to morrow the Lord will do wonders among you" (Joshua 3:5).

When we begin to move forward in service for the Lord we soon realize our need of divine strength. If we do not stay close to the Lord in prayer and Bible study, we will soon give up in discouragement in our attempts at soul winning.

Like ancient Israel, we are journeying to the

Promised Land. Like them, we are confronted with a seemingly impossible obstacle between where we are and our entrance into the heavenly kingdom. For us, it is the obstacle of an unfinished task. The character of Christ has not yet been perfectly reproduced in His people, and they have not yet carried the message of Good News to everyone everywhere.

These two prerequisites to entering the Promised Land are inseparably related to each other. "The great outpouring of the Spirit of God, which lightens the whole earth with His glory, will not come until we have an enlightened people, that know by experience what it means to be laborers together with God. When we have entire, wholehearted consecration to the service of Christ, God will recognize the fact by an outpouring of His Spirit without measure; but this will not be while the largest portion of the church are not laborers together with God."—*Christian Service*, p. 253.

> PRINCIPLE: *The majority of church members laboring cooperatively with God is a prerequisite to the latter rain.*

Spiritual Preparation

When we who claim to be God's people move out in obedient service for Him, we become more aware of our spiritual needs. At the same time, we qualify for a greater infilling of the Holy Spirit, which is given for service.

The power that piled up the waters of the Red Sea forty years before Jordan was the power that opened for the people of God a path through the river. The same God is ready to do wonders today if His people will be committed and willing to receive the sanctifying power of the Holy Spirit.

Waters in symbolic prophecy represent "peoples, and multitudes, and nations, and tongues" (Rev. 17:15). We would make an application and suggest that the figurative counterpart of the literal waters of the Jordan River in our day is the exploding population of our planet that must be reached with God's message of love before we can enter the heavenly Canaan. The "waters" that stand between where we are and where God wants us to be are people, not only the people of the world, but also the people of the church—you and me—in whose lives the Saviour is patiently posing for His portrait. Remember, we who are truly Christians become like Him as we share in His service. Indeed, this is a basic reason He has shared with us the privilege of service. "God could have reached His object in saving sinners without our aid; but in order for us to develop a character like Christ's, we must share in His work."—*Ibid.*, p. 8.

PRINCIPLE: *Christians become like Christ as they share in His work.*

God, then, can communicate His message without human instruments. He does not need us, but we all desperately need the involvement with Him in service. God could have performed a different type of miracle than He did to get the Israelites across the Jordan, but He chose a means that would test the faith of each individual. He gave them a seemingly impossible command, and not until they accepted the challenge did He miraculously intervene to open the way before them. There was no miracle until the people moved forward in response to God's call. Do you see the parallel for our day?

Sometimes, as members of the church, we think our assignment is impossible, and, humanly speaking, it is. When we consider becoming actively involved in a soul-winning project the devil presents many reasons why it is impossible—physical reasons, economic reasons, social reasons, and reasons of disposition. But when we do what is in our power to do, the miraculous power of God will do the rest.

Lay Preaching

Sarah Walker attended a lay preachers' institute and caught a vision of what could be done by the small, rural church of which she was a member. The inspiration she received at the institute revived memories of her youth in the West Indies. She remembered the group of laymen who banded together as a soul-winning team. One was the speaker, another had charge of the music, others looked after ushering, advertising, visitation, and so on.

Sarah was the only one from her little church to attend the institute. She went home fired with enthusiasm, certain that one of the men in the church would be willing to step into the role of lay preacher. But the men had not attended the institute. They had not caught the vision and the inspiration. Finally, in desperation, Sarah asked, "Will you support me if I do the preaching?" The church members assured her of their support.

It seemed impossible—a woman from the West Indies preaching in a conservative rural community with a 99 percent white population!

The meetings were held in a country schoolhouse. After two months of preaching and personal work, seven adults were baptized.

God knew that there was a harvest to be gathered in that little community. He arranged the timing of that lay preachers' institute and planned that Sarah Walker should be there to get the inspiration. God laid on her heart a burden, and she did something about it. Her actions opened the way for God to work and perform miracles of conversion.

The Mission

When Jesus gave the gospel commission to His little band of disciples, their reaction might easily have been—impossible! To go into all the wide world and preach the gospel to every creature could appear as a physical impossibility; the disciples did not have the means of transportation and communication available to us. It was a numerical impossibility; they were only a handful. It was a financial impossibility; they had no money or material possessions. It was a social impossibility; who would listen to these adherents of a new religion, and these followers of an unknown Jew, a Galilean carpenter?

But Jesus' followers had seen Him command a man with a withered arm, "Stretch forth thine hand" (Matt. 12:13). It looked impossible, but there was a power in the command that made it possible. Jesus' disciples had seen Him command a cripple who couldn't even stand on his feet, "Rise, take up thy bed, and walk" (John 5:8). This, too, seemed impossible, but once again, in the command of Jesus was the power that made it possible.

For a person knowing nothing about the principles of flight, it may seem impossible for a jumbo jet filled with passengers and cargo to leave the ground and fly through the air. But the laws of aerodynamics make the seemingly impossible possible.

When the sister of the Wright brothers received a telegram telling of their first successful flight, it included the message "Home for Christmas." She took the telegram to the editor of the local paper and told him about the flight. He looked at the telegram and said, "I'm so glad your brothers will be home for Christmas."

After she left, he turned to his associate and said, "Who does she think I am? Anyone knows that flying is impossible." That editor missed a news scoop because he was too quick to say, "Impossible."

The authority and validity of God's commands are important factors in accomplishing the seemingly impossible. The apostles accepted the command to witness "in Jerusalem, and in all Judaea, . . . and unto the uttermost part of the earth" (Acts 1:8) on the authority of their Lord. When they were brought before the Jewish leaders for following this command, they declared, "We ought to obey God rather than men" (chap. 5:29). Constrained by the love of Christ, they declared fearlessly "We are his witnesses" (verse 32). Verse 40 describes how they were beaten and commanded not to speak in the name of Jesus. However, there was a command from a higher authority, and the record says, "They ceased not to teach and preach Jesus Christ" (verse 42).

> PRINCIPLE: *There is a command to witness.*

The apostles who were stirred to action by Jesus'

command to witness were fishermen, tradesmen, and businessmen. They did not have the opportunity of receiving formal theological training, but they had the privilege of association with Jesus. That association impressed upon their minds the urgency of carrying the gospel to everyone, everywhere.

You and I have the privilege of spending time with Jesus in Bible study and prayer, and out of such communion will grow the conviction to do our part. Inspiration says, "The church must realize its obligation to carry the gospel of present truth to every creature."— *Ibid.*, p. 111.

"Got any rivers you think are uncrossable?
Got any mountains you can't tunnel through?
God specializes in things thought impossible,
And He can do what no other power can do."
—Oscar C. Eliason

Suggestions for Discussion

1 Discuss the ways in which the two prerequisites for entering the heavenly Canaan are interrelated.

2 God did not open a way through the waters until His people moved forward. Discuss the possible parallel in our day and experience.

3 Does Christ's assignment to the church to reach every creature seem impossible to you?

4 Discuss the thought that God could have communicated His message to the world without our aid. What are the implications of this statement?

5 What role could lay preaching play in the soul-winning program of your church?

43

6 Where in the Bible do we find the command to witness?

7 Does a proper emphasis of the command to witness lead to legalism more so than a similar emphasis on other commandments?

8 Can you now see how it is possible to accomplish the "impossible"?

9 What "impossible" soul would you like to win for Christ?

THE
JETHRO
PRINCIPLE

Jethro, the father-in-law of Moses, was a layman. He came to Moses with two penetrating questions: "What is this thing that thou doest to the people? why sittest thou thyself alone, and all the people stand by thee?" (Ex. 18:14).

Delegating Responsibility

Lay leaders in the church today can learn a valuable lesson from Jethro's questions. Without realizing it, Moses had been doing an injustice to the people by trying to do duties that should have been delegated to others. "The elders and those who have leading places in the church should give more thought to their plans for conducting the work. They should arrange matters so that every member of the church shall have a part to act, that none may lead an aimless life, but that all may accomplish what they can according to their several ability. . . . Let every member of the church become an active worker—a living stone, emitting light in God's temple."—*Christian Service*, p. 62.

> *PRINCIPLE: Church officers should delegate responsibility to members and teach them how to work for others.*

Building on his two questions, Jethro drew four conclusions:

1. "The thing that thou doest is not good."
2. "Thou wilt surely wear away."
3. "This thing is too heavy for thee."
4. "Thou are not able to perform it thyself alone" (Ex. 18:17, 18).

Similar counsel has come to the church in our day. "Those who have the spiritual oversight of the church should devise ways and means by which an opportunity may be given to every member of the church to act some part in God's work."—*Ibid.*, p. 61.

Jethro made four recommendations to his son-in-law:

1. "Be thou for the people to God-ward." (In other words, be God's representative.)
2. "Teach them . . . and . . . shew them the way."
3. Show them "the work that they must do."
4. "Provide . . . able men, . . . and place such over them, to be rulers." In other words, Moses was to delegate responsibility and authority (verses 19-22).

Three results that would come from following this advice were mentioned by Jethro:

1. "It [shall] be easier for thyself, and they shall bear the burden with thee."
2. "Thou shalt be able to endure."
3. "All this people shall also go to their place in peace" (verses 22, 23).

The Jethro principle applies at every level of leadership. It works in two directions; it prepares us to receive responsibility on the one hand and to divide and assign it on the other. It is a principle that should always be kept in mind by lay leadership in the church. Leaders should not attempt to do all the work themselves. Their duty is to organize the work, delegate responsibility and provide training and supervision.

There is a certain parallel between the Jethro principle, which provides for reception of responsibility, training of manpower, and the assignment of responsibility, and the principle as set forth by the apostle Paul in Ephesians 4:11, 12: "His gifts were that some should be apostles, some prophets, some evangelists, some pastors and teachers, for the equipment of the saints, for the work of ministry, for building up the body of Christ" (R.S.V.).

It is encouraging to see an ever-growing emphasis in the church on the importance of equipping and training church members for the work of ministry.

Every church leader would do well to note an incident described in *Christian Service* and to meditate on these words: " 'I employed you to keep six men at work. I found the six idle, and you doing the work of but one. Your work could have been just as well done by any one of the six. I cannot afford to pay the wages of seven for you to teach the six how to be idle.' "—Page 70.

In the parable of the vineyard those who were standing idle in the marketplace gave as the reason for their inactivity, "No man hath hired us" (Matt. 20:7). There is a great army of potential workers idle in our churches today simply because no one has assigned them to specific responsibilities and no one has taught them how to do the work. "Many would be willing to work if they were taught how to begin."—*Ibid.*, p. 59. Many are "idle in the market place," waiting to be assigned.

Hendrik Kraemer speaks of the untapped manpower in many congregations as "the frozen assets of the church."

On-the-Job Training

Oscar Gulley is a layman who became personally

concerned about these "frozen assets." Until he reached his early fifties he was one of those church members who gave the church generous financial support and reasoned that he was providing for others to do his share of soul-winning work. He had conditioned himself to automatically exclude himself when appeals were made for giving Bible studies or for any type of direct soul winning. The change came when the pastor approached him to accompany him on a Bible study.

"You won't have to say a thing," the pastor promised. "Just come along for moral support. I have a family I want some of our members to get acquainted with, and I'd like to begin with you, Oscar."

Week after week Oscar accompanied the pastor. It was a most revealing experience for him. He had always imagined that giving Bible studies required that one be a veritable walking encyclopedia of Biblical knowledge. He had also imagined that giving Bible studies was a battle of logic and debate, with the superior intellect ultimately winning. He found these presuppositions to be misconceptions. To his surprise he discovered that with the Bible knowledge he had gained from Sabbath school through the years, he would have been able to answer most of the questions the pastor was asked. On a few occasions he saw the pastor admit without embarrassment that he would have to research the matter during the week and bring the answer at the time of the next study. Oscar thought to himself, I could do that.

What made the greatest impression upon Oscar was the kindly interest the pastor took in the family. It was evident that he really loved people; he took an interest in each of the children and entered with a sympathetic spirit into the joys and sorrows of the little family.

Each week the conviction deepened in Oscar's mind that soul winning is basically loving people and attempting to relate to them as Jesus would if He were still here in the flesh.

I enjoy people. I believe I could learn to do what I've seen the pastor doing, Oscar reflected. And then he found himself reasoning, The pastor has at the most five evenings a week he can spend visiting families in this way—allowing for prayer meeting and at least one evening home with his family. If five church members would be willing to devote one evening a week to sharing their friendship with others and guiding them in Bible studies, we would have the equivalent of a second pastor so far as his evening activities are concerned.

Oscar discussed his idea with the pastor. He said, "I'll take my wife as my partner now. We'll take some of the names in the interest file and try to be friends to these people the way I've seen you doing it. We'll see if we can develop some Bible studies. And, pastor, may I suggest that you do for someone else in the church what you've done for me."

"What do you mean? What have I done for you?" the pastor asked.

"You've taken away my fear of the unknown by inviting me to go along and observe as you gave Bible studies," Oscar replied. "You've opened a new door of opportunity for me. I'm more excited about my relationship to Jesus and my membership in the church than I have been since I was baptized."

Discipling

In their first year as a friendship team sharing their love of Jesus with others, Oscar and his wife, Irene, led two of their contacts to decisions for Christ and to church membership. In four years that number had grown to twelve. At that point Oscar and Irene agreed on another step. "Let's make two teams," said Irene. "I'll find a woman in the church to go with me, and you can find a man to go with you, and each of us can start training disciples the way the pastor did with you."

Paul Benjamin, director of the National Church Growth Research Center, Washington, D.C., says, "The idea of every Christian being a minister for Christ has yet to dawn upon the American church."—*Christianity Today*, Sept. 22, 1978, p. 22.

Benjamin speaks of an "equipping ministry." Jesus was constantly seeking others who could minister. He spent much of His time equipping them to minister effectively. The apostle Paul followed a similar practice; he encouraged those whom he trained to seek others whom they could train. "And the things that thou hast heard of me among many witnesses, the same commit thou to faithful men, who shall be able to teach others also" (2 Tim. 2:2). This multiplication principle inherent in discipling has been the genius of the growth and spread of Christianity.

> PRINCIPLE: *By training those who will train others the working force will multiply.*

In the light of the foregoing statements, notice the counsel God has given us through the Spirit of Prophecy: "Many would be willing to work if they were taught how to begin. They need to be instructed and encouraged. Every church should be a training school for Christian workers. . . . There should not only be teaching, but actual work under experienced instructors. Let the teachers lead the way in working among the people, and others, uniting with them, will learn from their example."—*Christian Service,* p. 59.

> PRINCIPLE: *Every church should be a practical training school for "in-service training."*

In an interview for *Christianity Today,* Billy Graham was asked, " 'If you were a pastor in a large church in a principal city, what would be your plan of action?' Dr. Graham answered, 'I think one of the first things I would do would be to get a small group of 8 or 10 or 12 men around me that would meet a few hours a week and pay the price! It would cost them something in time and effort. . . . I would share with them everything I have, over a period of a couple of years. Then, I would actually have 12 ministers among the laymen, who in turn could take 8 or 10 or 12 more and teach them. I know one or two churches that are doing that, and it is revolutionizing the church. Christ, I think, set the pattern. He spent most of His time with 12 men. He didn't spend it with great crowds. In fact, every time He had a great crowd, it seems to me that there weren't too many results. The great results, it seems to me, came in His personal interviews and in the time He spent with His 12.' "— *Christianity Today,* Oct. 13, 1958, p. 5.

Following Jesus' Pattern

Dr. Graham said he knew a few churches that were following such a plan with good results. An increasing number of Seventh-day Adventist churches are following the plan. This shows a new awareness of the role the Bible describes for laymen in ministry. This is a pattern Jesus Himself established, and whenever we follow His example we know we are on the pathway to success.

"Passing by the self-righteous Jewish teachers, the Master Worker chose humble, unlearned men to proclaim the truths that were to move the world. These men He purposed to train and educate as the leaders of His church. They, in turn, were to educate others and send them out with the gospel message."—The Acts of the Apostles, p. 17.

Application of the Jethro principle will result in the division and delegation of responsibility through an undershepherd plan and the formation of small groups within the congregation. "The formation of small companies as a basis of Christian effort has been presented to me by One who cannot err."—Christian Service, p. 72.

These small companies could be Sabbath school classes. Ideally, each class should be a band of Christians planning, praying, and working for growth. Following nature's growth pattern of cell division, each class will divide and become two classes as soon as membership reaches a predetermined ceiling of twelve or so. The two resulting classes will then grow until they reach the dividing point. Such a process is automatically programmed in the natural world, but God has left it for human leaders to program this into our soul-winning work.

Spiritual Reproduction

There is a renewed interest in genealogy, or family trees, as people have become concerned about their "roots." What could be more fascinating than a spiritual family tree showing the reproduction of converts to the "fourth generation" or beyond, as illustrated in the diagram?

Spiritual Reproduction
The Case of Lucas

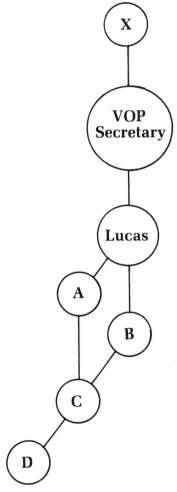

A girl on our VOP staff in Tanzania gave Bible studies to Lucas, who was just about to graduate from a theological seminary.

Within four months, Lucas had shared his faith, and two of his friends, represented by circles A and B, were baptized. A and B teamed together to work for the conversion of C, and after another four months, C was baptized.

C shared the message with D, and after four months, D was baptized.

Lucas is the spiritual son of the VOP secretary, A and B are grandchildren, C is the great-grandchild, and D is a great-great-grandchild, in a spiritual sense.

That is four generations of spiritual reproduction in the space of one year, and each may continue to reproduce.

If we knew the spiritual ancestry of the VOP secretary, we could chart this beginning with the one who shared the message with her in circle X and work back from there.

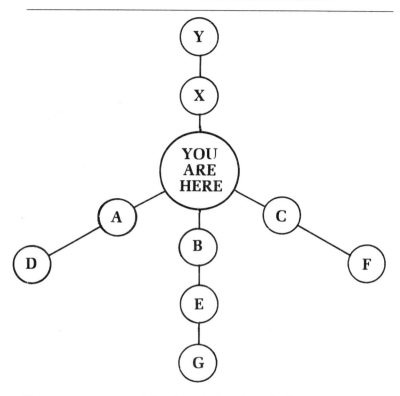

You are represented by the circle identified with the words "You Are Here."

By circle X put the name of the person who shared Christ and His truth with you. If you know who introduced that person to Christ, put that information by circle Y. Perhaps you can even trace your spiritual ancestry back beyond this.

If you have led others to Christ and baptism, put these names by circles A, B, and C. If you need more circles, make them.

If your converts have had spiritual children, list them by circles D, E, and F.

If you can trace additional generations of spiritual reproduction, add the necessary circles.

Emphasizing the importance of spiritual reproduction in the evangelistic strategy of our Lord, Robert E. Coleman says, "It did not matter how small the group was to start with, so long as they reproduced and taught their disciples to reproduce."—*The Master Plan of Evangelism,* p. 106.

Following this principle will cause little churches to grow into big churches. Neglecting this principle will cause small churches gradually to die.

Coleman goes on, "The Criteria upon which a church should measure its success is not how many new names are added to the role, nor how much the budget is increased, but rather, how many Christians are actively winning souls and training them to win the multitudes."—*Ibid.,* p. 110.

Thirty-five hundred years ago God communicated a principle through Jethro, a layman, which, if practiced, can help our churches to grow as we near the close of the twentieth century.

Suggestions for Discussion

1 In the case of Jethro sharing an idea with Moses, we have a situation akin to that of a layman sharing an idea with a pastor today. Discuss elements involved in a relationship like this, such as, respect for principles of church organization, good judgment, tact, patience.

2 Discuss reasons why enlisting participation on a one-to-one basis is more effective than calling for volunteers.

3 Discuss the misconceptions Oscar Gulley had about personal work and giving Bible studies.

4 What would you say was the most valuable lesson Oscar learned by accompanying his pastor?

5 How can you get the multiplication principle working in your church?

6 Analyze the statement from *Christian Service*, page 59, about every church being a training school. How many separate principles do you find in that paragraph?

7 What can you do as an individual church member about putting into operation the principle of small companies as a basis of Christian effort? Are you part of such a company?

THE MOMENTUM OF A MOVEMENT

The hymn writer captured the inspiration of the momentum of a movement when he penned the words "Like a mighty army Moves the church of God." This is God's ideal for His church. "The Lord Jesus desires the members of His church to be an army of workers."— *Medical Ministry*, p. 316.

God's plans for His church, like His plans for individuals, unfold gradually in stages. In the early decades of the Advent Movement the pioneers did not realize that their work must embrace the entire world. Many of them felt that Matthew 24:14 had already been fulfilled in one of two ways, either by being preached to representative peoples of all nations who had found a refuge in America or that it was being fulfilled in the world mission program of Protestantism in general.

God allowed time for a firm base to be established in North America before He beckoned Adventism to send missionaries to every nation. What has happened in the space of one hundred years or so since then is a miracle of modern missions. Adventists now have bases of operation in all but a very few countries listed by the United Nations, some of which are presently closed to Christian work for political reasons.

It now appears that God is once again sharpening the focus of our mission and beckoning us to take another step as His purpose for worldwide evangelization unfolds yet further. While for many years the emphasis was on reaching every nation, now the focus seems to be best expressed by Mark's version of the gospel commission, "To every creature" (Mark 16:15), or, as *The Living Bible* has it, "To everyone, everywhere." With deeper insight we read the words, "The church must realize its obligation to carry the gospel of present truth to every creature."—*Christian Service*, p. 111.

> PRINCIPLE: *The church has an obligation to present the gospel to every person.*

Gottfried Oosterwal reminds us that "though the Lord has never told us that the whole world will accept Him, He did definitely commission us to proclaim the gospel to every person on earth. Since Christ died for all of them, they all have a right to know it. Therein lies the challenge of our generation."—*Mission Possible*, p. 17.

To Every Man's Door

The thought of reaching everyone with a knowledge of Jesus and His message of good news may seem overwhelming. It might cause us to exclaim, Impossible! But, is our assignment any more impossible than the commission given to the original twelve disciples? We rejoice today that they did not respond, "Impossible!" Their experience reminds us that, "With God all things are possible" (Matt. 19:26).

A review of some trends will encourage each one of us. It is estimated that the population of the world at the time of Christ was in the neighborhood of 200 million. When Christ's followers numbered 12, the ratio was about one to 16.6 million.

When Christ sent out the 70, the ratio was one to 2,850,000.

When the number of believers had grown to 120, the ratio was one to 1,666,000.

After 3,000 believers were added on the Day of Pentecost, the ratio came down to one to 6,410 which was the ratio of Adventist members to world population in the year 1930.

Let's compare these figures with statistics for our day.

1900	1 SDA to every	20,460
1910	1 SDA to every	15,000
1920	1 SDA to every	9,760
1930	1 SDA to every	6,410
1940	1 SDA to every	4,450
1950	1 SDA to every	3,300
1960	1 SDA to every	2,240
1970	1 SDA to every	1,730
1980	1 SDA to every	1,250

Now, allowing an average of three persons to every dwelling, less than 500 households need to be contacted by each Seventh-day Adventist. This is not impossible, even humanly speaking. We realize that simply making a contact is not all that is involved in bringing the light of the gospel to an individual, but because this is God's work, to be accompanied with His promised power, we are not left with only human resources. As a matter of fact, God is but waiting for a committed people seriously to attempt what we might consider an impossible task. Then He will intervene with His miracle-working power to bring about its accomplishment.

Please reread those last two sentences. So far as the words of the author are concerned, they are probably the most important in this book. Their basis lies in the following paragraph: "When we have entire, whole-hearted consecration to the service of Christ, God will recognize the fact by an outpouring of His Spirit without measure; but this will not be while the larger portion of the church are not laborers together with God."—*Christian Service*, p. 253.

God longs for the church to be a loving, sharing, serving fellowship. It is only as we join the Saviour in service that we shall come to reflect His character. The Lord wants us to know the life-transforming joy that is to be found in soul-saving ministry.

Too often we bog down in discussions over the feasibility of taking the gospel to every living person. This is no problem to God. His problem is to get us ready for citizenship in His kingdom. Inspiration says He can do this only by involving us in His service. Such service cannot be forced. It must be a voluntary response of love for God and His creatures.

A willingness to become involved in soul-saving service is a byproduct of genuine conversion, but it remains the responsibility of the church to provide the organization and the training.

In North America, the ratio is approximately one Adventist to 500 non-SDAs. This means fewer than two hundred homes to be reached by the influence of each Seventh-day Adventist. But there is more good news. Many of these homes have already been reached by the radio, television, or literature outreach of the church. Many of the names of the 500 are already in the interest files of the local church. We can go to their homes not as strangers but as friends, to follow up the interest triggered by the media.

In most cases it is only when the names in the prospect file have been exhausted that we begin a door-to-door ministry. This also can be an enjoyable and rewarding experience.

A Serving Fellowship

Think of the possibilities of a door-to-door ministry patterned after the example of Jesus. "Our Saviour went from house to house, healing the sick, comforting the mourners, soothing the afflicted, speaking peace to the disconsolate."—*Ibid.*, p. 114.

> PRINCIPLE: Jesus went from house to house.

Christ's method is not a combative, argumentative approach, but rather an approach of loving service, meeting felt human needs. This is denoted in the words used in the preceding statement—healing, comforting, soothing, and speaking peace to the disconsolate.

Christ's model does not lead to a stereotyped, mechanical approach, but to loving ministry in harmony with the varied gifts and talents possessed by the members of His church.

In these sophisticated days there is a tendency on the part of many to turn away from house-to-house work. We can see why the enemy of souls would encourage such an attitude when we read that "this house-to-house labor, searching for souls, hunting for the lost sheep, is the most essential work that can be done."—*Evangelism*, p. 431. We have been commissioned to "carry the Word of God to every man's door" (*Christian Service*, p. 144).

> PRINCIPLE: House-to-house labor is the most essential work that can be done.

There is a tendency to feel that only certain ones can do house-to-house work. However, when we recognize that there are as many ways for evangelizing a community as there are differing spiritual gifts, we begin to see matters in a new light.

Perhaps the problem has been that we have had a tendency to think of house-to-house work in terms of a one-time visit to deliver a warning with a take-it-or-leave-it attitude, or as an attempt to force our religious beliefs on others. The concept of door-to-door ministry promoted in this book is that of sharing good news, meeting human needs, and putting love into action. It is not a cold, mechanical, dutiful checking off of house numbers, but rather it includes a friendly visit to the neighbor, a welcome to the newcomer, a listening ear for the lonely, and a pot of soup for the family with a sick wife and mother.

Behind the expression "house to house" we must think of the human needs behind the doors—needs that we will never be aware of until we reach those doors, needs that will challenge us to draw closer to Jesus so that we may be able to minister His love to those who need it so desperately.

Within this broader concept of visitation there is room for the involvement of every member. "Wherever a church is established, all the members should engage actively in missionary work. They should visit every family in the neighborhood, and know their spiritual condition."—*Ibid.*, p. 12.

PRINCIPLE: *"All the members should engage actively in missionary work."*

As we ponder these words, God's plan becomes clearer. It is not His plan that a minority of church members, who make up the traditional missionary band, should be left alone with this task. Can we expect a minority to work with enthusiasm while the majority remain idle? Certainly this is not God's ideal. God's plan is that every member should take part in different ways.

Experience has revealed at least two ways of moving in the direction of God's ideal of majority involvement. The first way is based on individual initiative and the contagion of joyful success resulting in the multiplication of small groups. This we have already discussed at some length.

New Convert Involvement

The other approach is based on the assignment emphasis found in the inspired writings. "Every one who is added to the ranks by conversion is to be assigned his post of duty."—*Ibid.*, p. 74.

> PRINCIPLE: *New converts are to be assigned a post of duty.*

One church—we'll call it the Springbrook church—became very interested in the principle in this inspired statement. With the encouragement of their local elder and the approval of the district pastor, they decided to follow this simple directive from the Lord. But they also reasoned that if every new convert was to receive an assignment, to set the right example the other members should have assignments too. They also decided that the assignments would be given on a territorial basis. They reasoned this way:

At every level of organization in the Seventh-day Adventist Church there are definite territorial boundaries with specific individuals responsible for the work in that area. The world field is subdivided into divisions, the divisions into unions, and the unions into local conferences or fields. The local fields are subdivided into districts, with every church within a district having its specific territory. The pastor cannot possibly reach all the people in the church territory. The command to witness applies to every believer. Every believer is a minister, and therefore it seems reasonable that every believer, or at least every family, should have a specific territorial responsibility.

This reasoning seemed to find support in many Spirit of Prophecy statements, including the one that says, "Not all can go as missionaries to foreign lands, but all can be home missionaries in their families and neighborhoods."—*Christian Service*, p. 9.

Further incentive was given to the Springbrook church to have family territory when a comment by Dr. Oosterwal was noted: "Because Adventists have failed to enlist all their members in mission, the work has remained unfinished."—*Mission Possible*, p. 64.

Lester Russell, one of the members of the Springbrook church, was sightless. When he heard enthusiastic conversations about the assignment of missionary territory to each family in the church, he was fearful that he might be left out because of his blindness. So he contacted the local elder and suggested he would like to have territory close to the church; he felt he could make some visits after the service each Sabbath. His request was granted, and each Sabbath you could see him with his white cane feeling his way through his territory.

Lester decided to use a traditional literature approach. With a smile for people he couldn't see, and a cheery word for everybody, he was able to have his literature accepted at most homes. Not all the recipients read it, but some did. One woman in the block next to the church developed such a deep interest through the literature left by Lester that she began attending Sabbath services, experienced true conversion, and was baptized. As a new member, she was given a mission territory in harmony with the counsel, "When souls are converted, set them to work at once."—*Evangelism*, p. 355.

There was something contagious about this woman's experience with the Lord, and it wasn't long before she interested another woman in her territory. She is now baptized and working for others. This is another illustration of spiritual reproduction. The chain reaction goes on. And it all started because a blind man was willing to be assigned a post of duty.

We'll read more about the Springbrook church in the next chapter. As you read, you'll be interested in a few details of just how they launched their territorial program. Their experience certainly bears out the fact that "if the proper instruction were given, if the proper methods were followed, every church member would do his work as a member of the body. He would do Christian missionary work."—*Ibid.*, p. 381.

Think of the possibilities if everyone added to church membership was truly converted and eager to reach others. "If every church member had sought to enlighten others, thousands upon thousands would today stand with God's commandment-keeping people."—*Welfare Ministry*, p. 72.

New believers, inspired by their first-love experience, are often the most willing workers. They usually have friends and relatives who have observed the change conversion has brought to their lives. Some of these may prove to be excellent prospects. New members should be given guidance and encouragement to begin working for souls immediately after their conversion, and should have the inspiration that comes from knowing that their brothers and sisters in the church are working too. A tremendous sense of fulfillment comes when one belongs to an organization in which the majority are working with a spirit of dedication for a common objective. United effort gives purpose and the promise of a finished task. This is the momentum of a movement.

Your Mission Field

"They [all the members] should visit every family in the neighborhood, and know their spiritual condition."— *Christian Service*, p. 12.

Make a diagram of your neighborhood. Draw in the houses or apartments of your ten nearest neighbors. Do you know their spiritual condition? If not, how many?

Think of the needs and interests of each of the ten and outline a strategy for developing a friendship with each and, when the time is right, acquainting them with Christ and His message.

Include the names of these ten neighbors on your prayer list.

"All can be missionaries in their families and neighborhoods."—*Ibid.*, p. 9.

Suggestions for Discussion

1 Discuss the sentence, "The church must realize its obligation to carry the gospel of

present truth to every creature."—*Christian Service*, page 111. Has your church really come to grips with this obligation? Do you have a plan to reach everyone in your church's territory?

2 Divide the Adventist membership into the total population within your conference to find the ratio of Adventists to non-Adventists. Do the same for your church territory if figures are available.

3 Why, as a general rule, should the people whose names are in the interest file be visited before going door-to-door looking for prospects?

4 Discuss the challenge of knowing the spiritual condition of every family in the church territory. How can this be done?

5 What are some activities a new believer can engage in?

6 Surveys reveal that soul-winning productivity tends to decline after one has been a member more than three years. What do you think is the reason for this?

7 What more can we do to move closer to God's ideal for new-member involvement as emphasized in the Spirit of Prophecy?

FASTEN YOUR MIND ON A SOUL

The Springbrook church board decided to have an assignment Sabbath during which each family would receive its own subdivision of the total church territory. This plan was conceived as a means of helping the church toward the ideal God envisioned when He directed that each new convert should be assigned a post of duty. The board decided on territorial assignments on the basis of the Spirit of Prophecy counsel that "wherever a church is established, all the members should engage actively in missionary work. They should visit every family in the neighborhood, and know their spiritual condition."—*Christian Service*, p. 12.

A check of the church membership list of 194 showed that there were 78 families who could be assigned territorial responsibility. This excluded three shut-ins who would be assigned as prayer partners to team up with other members.

Any time several people join in visiting every home in a given area, there must be a plan; there must be organization. It is not enough simply to say, "Go and share the good news." Certainly we should do that at every opportunity, but if we are to reach every person with the good news, we must have a plan.

"God is a God of order. Everything connected with heaven is in perfect order; subjection and thorough discipline mark the movements of the angelic hosts. Success can only attend order and harmonious action. God requires order and system in His work now no less than in the days of Israel. All who are working for Him are to labor intelligently, not in a careless, haphazard manner."—*Ibid.*, p. 73.

Wisely, right from the planning stages, the Springbrook church board involved as many members as possible in its project. A church business meeting was scheduled for Sabbath afternoon following a fellowship dinner. There was only one item on the agenda: finishing the work. Small groups discussed such questions as:

1. Does every member have some spiritual gift that can be exercised in soul-winning outreach?

2. Do church officers have the right to assign soul-winning duties, or should all such activity be on a voluntary basis?

3. How can we reach every non-SDA family in our territory and know their spiritual condition?

4. Can every converted, able-bodied member be a missionary in his neighborhood?

5. Does Mark 16:15 literally mean that every person must be reached with the gospel?

6. Is there a command to witness resting on a basis similar to the command to keep the Sabbath and to be baptized?

The group brainstorming sessions generated an enthusiastic spirit that was obvious as each group reported on its discussions. The reports were followed by a time of prayer, testimonies, and claiming of God's promises. The local elder proposed dividing the church territory among the families of the church, and all the members expressed their agreement with this plan.

Territorial Assignment

Actually six weeks of planning had prepared the way for assignment Sabbath. The decision had been made to give each family two territories, so two identical maps of the entire church territory were obtained. Identical boundaries were traced on each map. The entire territory was divided into 156 subdivisions, providing a home territory and a "mission" territory for each of 78 families. There were two reasons for the arrangement: the desire to give each family a territory close to their home, and a concern to reach the more distant areas of the church territory.

In planning the territories, careful thought had to be given to the circumstances of the individual church families. Actually, some consisted of a single individual. Others included parents and children.

Two maps were necessary because one was to be kept intact for the permanent church records. The other was cut into segments as indicated by the territorial boundaries. The numbers assigned to the territories made it possible for the lay activities council to keep a record of the family assigned to any given territory.

When the work on the map was completed, the church copy was displayed for two Sabbaths, giving the members an opportunity to indicate their choice of territory by writing their name and the number of the territory selected on a pad placed by the map. The majority of church members chose to allow the church leaders to make the decision.

Our Territory

You could think of your family territory as an inheritance of land—a farm. You choose a spot for a garden. Here you will plant seed, cultivate, and finally

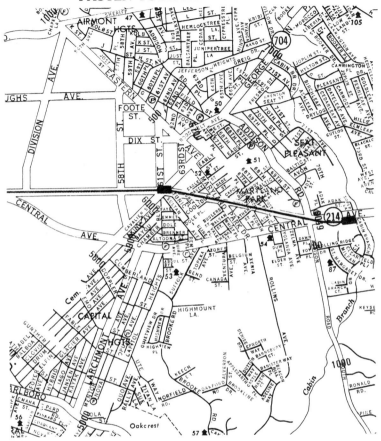

gather a harvest. In addition you might discover an oil well or a gold mine. These represent people whose initial interest springs from some source other than your labors. They might have had their interest sparked by a radio or TV program or by reading Adventist literature. They are yours to follow up because they are in your territory. The larger your territory the more such prospects you may expect to find.

During the weeks of preparation the Springbrook

church interest coordinator made a duplicate of each name in the church interest file. These were sorted according to boundaries and given to the members with their territorial packet. This plan would go a long way toward making provision for the follow-up of media and literature interests.

The members of the church found special satisfaction in the realization that the entire territory around their church was divided and assigned. The importance of prayer was emphasized in carrying out the plan, so the members knew that every person living within the church territory would be the object of special prayer on the part of some Seventh-day Adventist family.

Assignment Sabbath was a very special day at the Springbrook church. The pastor preached a deeply spiritual message dealing with the unfinished work in individual lives, as well as the challenge of carrying the gospel "to every man's door." As the climax of this special worship service, a representative from each family went forward to receive the family territory map. The pastor read Bible and Spirit of Prophecy statements dealing with the gospel commission while the organ played softly. It was inspiring to see the members go forward. Several had tears in their eyes.

Four stations had been set up at the front of the sanctuary, each identified alphabetically, A-G, H-M, et cetera, and manned by two church members. The other members quietly went to the station with the letter corresponding with the family name. To avoid any possible embarrassment, each quietly said, "My name is ————." He was handed the proper folder containing the portions of the map comprising their two territories, an Every Member Personal Territory Guide booklet (available from the Department of Lay Activities), and the names from the church interest file with addresses in their territory.

Intercessory Prayer

In his sermon the pastor made it clear that the success of the project would depend upon prayer. "All that we ask of you initially is to accept a territory and begin praying for the people in it," he said. "If we ask you to give Bible studies or distribute literature some of you will say, 'I can't do it.' But every Adventist can pray, and there is tremendous power in intercessory prayer."

The pastor knew that if his members would faithfully maintain a prayer ministry something would happen in their own lives, as well as in the lives of those for whom they were praying. Inspiration says, "He who does nothing but pray, will soon cease to pray."—*Steps to Christ*, p. 101.

"Begin to pray for souls; come near to Christ, close to His bleeding side. Let a meek and quiet spirit adorn your lives, and let your earnest, broken, humble petitions ascend to Him for wisdom that you may have success in saving not only your own soul, but the souls of others."—*Testimonies*, vol. 1, p. 513.

> PRINCIPLE: *"He who does nothing but pray, will soon cease to pray."*

There were exciting developments in the Springbrook church following assignment Sabbath. Things began to happen that very day. Typical of the enthusiasm displayed by many of the older church members was that of a preschool-age boy who came to the pastor at the close of the service carrying a brown paper grocery sack. "This is what I'm going to use in my territory!" said the little fellow with great enthusiasm, pointing to some neatly rolled left-over literature from his division of the Sabbath school.

Small groups of members tarried on the sidewalk after the church service, discussing plans for their territorial exploits. A successful businessman was heard to say approvingly, "I like this businesslike approach to the work of the Lord." And after all, God's work is the most important business there is.

The system followed by the Springbrook church removes the uncertainty of whether someone else might be working in an area and thus eliminates the embarrassment of overlap on the one hand or neglect on the other.

The prayers of the members became increasingly more specific. One family began by praying, "Please bless the people who live between Broadway and Main Street and between 37th and 69th, because that's our territory." This family added to their prayer list the specific names from the interest file of people living in their territory.

Fasten Your Mind on a Soul

Prayers become increasingly more specific:

"Bless the people in our territory."

"Bless the people who live between Broadway and Main Street and between 37th and 69th, because that's our territory."

"Bless the Jackson family on Maple Street."

"Please convict the Jackson family of their need for Christ. Help Mr. Jackson with his Sabbath work problem."

As the names of other interested people reached the church interest coordinator from various sources, they were channeled to the proper families, who immediately added them to the family prayer list. The next step was a friendship visit to get acquainted.

Family Togetherness in Soul Winning

In some cases two or three families chose to work their territories together. This made possible variations in visiting teams and increased the opportunity for learning experiences. In addition to the husband and wife team, two husbands were able to visit together, or two wives or two teen-age young people. Smaller children enjoyed accompanying their parents in visitation. This is the ideal way for young people to learn from childhood in a very natural way the art of sharing their faith.

An emphasis on spiritual gifts was effectively blended with territorial assignment at the Springbrook church. Church leaders offered many suggestions as to what might be done within the family territories, but the final strategy was left with the individual families. The local elder wisely observed, "If we prematurely ask a member to do something he does not feel ready or prepared to do, we will only hurt the program."

The prayer emphasis was brought home to the members each week in Sabbath school, in the lay activities period, and in the worship service. They responded to the challenge, "In times past there were those who fastened their minds upon one soul after another, saying, 'Lord, help me to save this soul.' But now such instances are rare. How many act as if they realized the peril of sinners?"—*Gospel Workers*, p. 65.

The ministry of prayer served to motivate the

members. One family after another began an outreach. Some began by visiting the ill and the elderly in their territories. Others cultivated the friendship of their neighbors. Still others made their initial contacts by delivering service-type information, such as announcements of Vacation Bible Schools, cooking schools, Five-Day Plans and Community Services center information.

The number one emphasis was always prayer. The next priority was following up existing prospects from the interest file. The visits are usually relatively easy because the people have already had some contact with our teachings and have manifested some degree of interest.

Realizing the value of small-group dynamics, the Springbrook church leaders made provision for the lay activities service to be conducted in the Sabbath school class units at least three weeks out of each month. The ten-minute period became an exciting time of sharing experiences and laying plans for future outreach. At first some of the members were concerned about visitors' reactions if they were exposed to this type of soul-winning planning. Let me tell you about one visitor.

Margaret Bell had become interested in Adventism through listening to the Voice of Prophecy, and she had completed a Bible correspondence course. Although she was a member of another Protestant church, she had thought seriously of visiting the Adventist church. One Friday, listening to the daily Voice of Prophecy program, she heard H.M.S. Richards invite listeners to visit their nearest Adventist church the next day. It was just the motivation that Margaret needed. She was one of the first to arrive for Sabbath school at the Springbrook church the next morning, and she greatly enjoyed the Sabbath school class. At the conclusion of the lesson study, she listened to the class members enthusiastically telling about the experiences they had had during the week sharing the love of Jesus in their territories. They told of comforting the lonely, praying with the frustrated, and offering Bible studies to those who were longing for a deeper understanding of the Word of God.

Margaret appreciated the worship service that followed, and began attending the church regularly. After her baptism several months later she commented that while everything impressed her favorably that Sabbath, the thing that made the deepest impression was the joy and enthusiasm of the members as they told how they were ministering to human needs in their territories. "That is practical Christianity. This is the type of activity I would like to take part in," she said.

Some members of the Springbrook church had soul-winning projects before territorial assignment was introduced. The majority of these continued with renewed fervor. They experienced a greater sense of participation in the soul-winning program now that they had their own territories. There were a few who were already actively involved who did not see why they needed specific territories. Among these was a physician who was actively giving Bible studies. He had all the prospects he could handle from among his patients. They were scattered over the city, and he could not see why he should have a specific territory under these circumstances. His attitude changed completely when the following points were called to his attention:

1. No one was suggesting that he should neglect existing interests to search for other prospects.

2. The territorial concept is flexible enough to allow the professional person to follow up contacts regardless of geographical location. (All that is necessary is to mention the contact to the one who has that territory).

3. The physician's wife and children should not be

denied the privilege of joining in the church program in the same way other families do.

4. The physician and his family could undertake a prayer responsibility for a given territory.

5. There is a detrimental psychological effect when exceptions are made. In unity there is strength (and inspiration!)

As territorial assignment became an established way of life in the Springbrook church, a great deal of interchange within one another's territories developed. Some, because of their professions or businesses, made contact with prospects within a wider circle than their assigned territory. These always had the privilege of following up their prospects regardless of territorial boundaries. In actual practice the entire church became a resource bank from which the appropriate talent could be drawn to best work with individual cases. Members who spoke languages other than English were a valuable help for interested people who did not speak English. In some cases, church members found people who were deaf or blind. Certain members, because of background or interest, specialized in those areas. It was beautiful to see the spirit of cooperation that developed as church members went all out to help one another in their territorial projects.

In cities with many Adventist churches the division of territory is admittedly more difficult than in a city with only one church. This can be resolved by representatives from each church meeting to work out interchanges of territory where necessary. Usually, because of Ingathering and literature distribution activities, church territories have already been divided. We must remember that the commission to reach everyone is from God and not just a plan of man's devising.

Businessmen have found ways to deliver merchandise to every home. Utilities workers managed to find and read every meter. The postal service manages to deliver messages from person to person in every part of the world by dividing territory and assigning responsibility to specific individuals. Certainly the leaders of God's church, commissioned to communicate a message from God to man, can make no less effort to deliver the Bread of Life.

"The church of Christ on earth was organized for missionary purposes, and the Lord desires to see the entire church devising ways and means whereby high and low, rich and poor, may hear the message of truth."—*Testimonies*, vol. 6, p. 29.

Fasten your mind on a soul and then seek the Lord for wisdom as you devise ways and means to win that soul for Christ and His message. Do this with one after another in your territory and God will make Himself responsible for the results.

Suggestions for Discussion

1 Discuss the six questions taken up in the Sabbath afternoon meeting at the Springbrook church.

2 Make a list of the advantages you see in the territorial assignment plan.

3 Discuss the advantages of two or more families working together in their territories.

4 Discuss the advantages of children participating from an early age with their parents in soul-winning activities.

5 Discuss the advantages of conducting the lay activities period in small groups such as Sabbath school classes.

6 Discuss how the assignment concept can benefit other church activities. List the activities you think should benefit.

7 List other projects or activities than those suggested that could be carried on by members in their territories.

8 Territorial assignment has resulted in an increase of lay involvement in many churches. What reasons can you think of to account for this?

9 Sometimes we are reluctant to discuss soul-winning methods and plans in the presence of non-SDA visitors. What does the story of Margaret Bell suggest in this connection?

10 Why do you think relatively more growth occurs in small groups?

11 Do you have territorial assignment in your church?

12 If you do, what methods are you following to reach the people in your territory?

REASONABLE SERVICE

"I beseech you therefore, brethren, by the mercies of God, that ye present your bodies a living sacrifice, holy, acceptable unto God, which is your reasonable service" (Rom. 12:1). Jesus asks for the unreserved service of our bodies—our hands, our feet, our tongues—to communicate His love to mankind. He has paid in advance for this service. We are "bought with a price" (1 Cor. 6:20). He purchased us "with his own blood" (Acts 20:28). It is therefore most reasonable that He should ask for our service.

Following World War I a sculptor offered to restore a damaged statue of Christ that stood in front of a church in Germany. Both hands of the statue had been destroyed. But after considering the matter, the congregation voted to leave the statue without hands to convey the message that Christ depends on our hands to do His work.

"Christ has no hands but our hands
    To do His work today;
He has no feet but our feet
    To lead men in His way;
He has no tongue but our tongue
    To tell men how He died,
He has no help but our help
    To bring them to His side."
        —Annie Johnson Flint

81

While our services should be available to our Lord at any moment of opportunity, observation has demonstrated that there will be more spontaneous witness when experience has been gained through organized, planned witness. A reasonable amount of service could probably be rendered by most of us during two hours a week. Think of the possibilities if every believer would consistently dedicate this minimum time to the task of sharing the good news with people in his territory. With the diversity of talents and spiritual gifts in the church, we can imagine that this time would be used in many different ways. Some would use it for getting better acquainted with their neighbors. "Go to your neighbors one by one, and come close to them till their hearts are warmed by your unselfish interest and love. Sympathize with them, pray with them, watch for opportunities to do them good. . . . Do not neglect speaking to your neighbors, and doing them all the kindness in your power, that you 'by all means may save some.' "—*Christian Service*, p. 116.

Some would watch for opportunities to invite neighbors into their homes, perhaps to teach them sewing, or to demonstrate vegetarian cooking, or to share a wholesome meal. We entertain guests from faraway places. We might be surprised at the results if we were to show similar hospitality to some of our neighbors. If we would invite more people into our homes, it would be easier to invite them to our church.

In areas where there is a shifting population a visit to newcomers is a welcome, pleasant, profitable, and easy type of contact. People who have moved and left behind friends and relatives are usually very receptive to a friendship type of visit. We will meet the rich and the poor, and both classes need what we have to offer—the love of Jesus.

"Many in high social positions are heart-sore, and sick of vanity. They are longing for a peace which they have not. In the very highest ranks of society are those who are hungering and thirsting for salvation. Many would receive help if the Lord's workers would approach them personally, with a kind manner, a heart made tender by the love of Christ."— *Ibid.*, p. 204.

"There are multitudes struggling with poverty. . . . When pain and sickness are added, the burden is almost insupportable. Careworn and oppressed, they know not where to turn for relief. Sympathize with them in their trials, their heartaches, and disappointments. This will open the way for you to help them. Speak to them of God's promises, pray with and for them, inspire them with hope."—*Ibid.*, p. 189.

An Adventist pastor, talking with a chaplain of the State hospital in a northern State, was told that if Christians would visit and comfort troubled people who eventually end up in a mental institution, many of them would find a way out of their distress without having to be committed. The chaplain concluded his remarks with the words, "If only Christians would visit!"

Many people are desperately lonely and need someone who will listen with a sympathetic ear. Many are without hope. They don't know how to pray. They need the very kind of help that Christians should be able to share. Every case of suicide raises the question, Could that life have been saved had some Christian but taken time to visit and be a friend?

"Many have gone down to ruin who might have been saved if their neighbors, common men and women, had put forth personal effort for them. Many are waiting to be personally addressed. In the very family, the neighborhood, the town, where we live, there is work for us to do as missionaries for Christ."—*The Desire of*

Ages, p. 141. Certainly this is a challenging appeal for reasonable service. Think again of the possibilities of reserving two hours a week for this kind of activity.

Receptivity

In working with our neighbors, we should be careful not to come on too strongly. A gentle approach usually works best. It is important to win their friendship and confidence first. In some cases this might take considerable time, especially where there is prejudice.

After their friendship has been won, we should patiently watch for natural opportunities to introduce spiritual themes in a tactful way. This is following Christ's example.

Receptivity varies with circumstances. We need to watch patiently for receptive moods. To scratch where there's no itch only causes irritation.

There is no relish for food when one is not hungry. People need to become aware of the questions before they will appreciate the answers. It is largely the work of the Holy Spirit to create desire and a sense of need. With experience we will learn how we may become sensitive to cooperating with the Holy Spirit.

Common mistakes of novice personal workers include:

1. Mistaking kindness and courtesy for interest in spiritual things.

2. Spending much time with a zealous adherent of another faith whose motive is really to convert the worker to his way of thinking.

3. Devoting all available time to religious friends who are perfectly satisfied with their own churches.

4. Neglecting those who appear to be irreligious.

5. Failing to distinguish between fruit that is ripe and fruit that is green.

Indicators of genuine interest include,

1. The asking of sincere questions.
2. Faithfulness in meeting Bible-study appointments.
3. Evidences of change in the life, and a response to truth that has been learned.
4. Respect for spiritual things.
5. A desire to share with others that which has been learned.
6. Willingness to attend Sabbath school and church.

Recognizing Interest

Generally speaking, the best prospects are people who do not have strong attachments to another church. They are not so likely to be steeped in error that must be unlearned. Remember, you can't fill a cup that is already

Truth cannot be forced into a mind that is already filled with error. It is the work of the Holy Spirit to dislodge error and create a thirst for truth.

The receptivity of individuals may vary greatly from one visit to another, depending upon altering circumstances. We must work in cooperation with the Holy Spirit.

full. To attempt to impart truth to one whose mind is filled with error may cause hostility in him and bring frustration to you.

"Christ drew the hearts of His hearers to Him by the manifestation of His love, and then, little by little, as they were able to bear it, He unfolded to them the great truths of the kingdom. We also must learn to adapt our labors to the condition of the people—to meet men where they are."—*Evangelism*, p. 484.

Some church members doing missionary work have alienated people by bringing up controversial subjects prematurely. Jesus used great tact in all His work. The Spirit of Prophecy counsels us, "You should not feel it your duty to introduce arguments upon the Sabbath question as you meet the people. If persons mention the subject, tell them that this is not your burden now. But when they surrender heart and mind and will to God, they are then prepared candidly to weigh evidence in regard to these solemn, testing truths."—*Ibid.*, p. 485.

Service approaches provide a very pleasant way to work the family territory. Sometimes two or three families will choose to cooperate in conducting a Five-Day Plan to Stop Smoking or a cooking class. A non-Adventist husband in an affluent neighborhood proposed to his church-member wife that they have a Five-Day Plan in their home and invite interested neighbors to come. The project proved very successful. Several Five-Day Plans have since been held, resulting in the establishment and cultivation of many new friendships.

Delivering invitations to Five-Day Plans, cooking classes, Vacation Bible Schools, et cetera, are service-type visits that are generally well received and provide a simple yet effective means of getting acquainted with families in our territories.

Books, Magazines, Cassettes

Some will choose more traditional methods such as literature distribution or the use of Bible correspondence enrollment cards. A congregation we will call the Apple Valley church has for many years had consistently good harvests from the systematic distribution of *Signs of the Times*. Each month a club of several hundred magazines is neatly arranged on the rostrum for a special service of prayer before members take them to their territories. The monthly delivery to people willing to receive and read them develops many friendships. Interested readers are enrolled in the Gift Bible Plan and later invited to the pastor's Sabbath school class or to evangelistic meetings.

The lending library method is still effective. There are books gathering dust on the shelves of many Adventist homes that could be a blessing if put into circulation through a lending library plan. This is especially true of missionary and other story books that are easy to read and yet useful in developing an interest in the message.

Some lay workers use cassettes with good results. Tom Berry, a young man who left the Midwest and went to California in search of a fortune, was enterprising and energetic and prospered financially. If you could talk to him today, however, he would tell you that the true fortune he found was not in silver and gold but rather in Jesus Christ and His teachings. Tom met a Seventh-day Adventist layman in California who loved the Lord and revealed His joy in his daily living. Tom caught what his friend had and has been spreading it to others ever since. The last time I talked to Tom he had a lending library of a thousand cassettes—Bible studies and evangelistic sermons. He uses a very simple approach, something like this: "Do you have a cassette player?" If the answer is Yes, he produces a cassette and says, "I have something here I think you'll enjoy. I'll stop by next week and pick it up."

If the individual does not have a cassette player, he offers to lend one. He has purchased two dozen for this purpose.

When Tom returns the next week he greets his prospect with a cheery "How did you like the cassette I left with you last week?" In the majority of cases the response is positive. Tom then produces another cassette. Many of his prospects listen to several a week, but he tries to keep them on a program of at least one a week. In many cases the borrowers listen to a cassette over and over and share it with friends. Often they do not want to part with it but offer to buy it.

Every few months I receive a phone call from Tom, who bubbles over with enthusiasm as he tells me of another baptism resulting from his cassette ministry.

One of the easiest ways of getting acquainted with people, making them friends, and learning their spiritual condition is the use of the Community Religious Survey. Perhaps the most widely used survey today is that found on page 171. About 80 percent of those contacted are willing to complete it.

Details of how to take the survey and how to make an easy transition to the offer of Bible reading guides are found in the Appendix on pages 167 and 168.

If you follow one or more of the above approaches, before long you will discover that the two hours set aside each week for missionary work will be needed for Bible study visits. New life and new members will come into any church whose members are dedicating a minimum of two hours a week to such outreach ministry. As we unselfishly work for others, our spiritual experience prospers, and we become more like Jesus. We have the promise that "when the churches become living, working churches, the Holy Spirit will be given in answer to their sincere request. . . . Then the windows of heaven will be open for the showers of the latter rain."—Ellen G. White, in *Review and Herald*, Feb. 25, 1890.

When the majority of church members perform their reasonable service by seriously attempting the seemingly impossible task of reaching everyone, everywhere, God's miracle-working power will come into play.

A family was preparing to move into a new home. The father was helping the movers carry the furniture and packing boxes into the truck as his little boy watched and wondered. Typical of little boys, he wanted to help. Walking over to a box much larger than himself he tried to lift it but couldn't even move it. The father saw his son's efforts, so, coming up behind him, he put his arms around the boy and the box and carried them together into the moving van. As the father set his load down, the little boy looked into his face with pride and exclaimed, "We did it, Father, didn't we!" And the father replied, "Yes, my child, we did."

What a beautiful picture of how the work is going to be finished. God has asked us to take the gospel to every creature. It seems such a superhuman task, but God is watching. When He sees that we are putting all our strength—our whole heart and mind and soul into the work—He will reach down with power from above, and "when divine power is combined with human effort, the work will spread like fire in the stubble" (*Selected Messages*, book 1, p. 118).

Suggestions for Discussion

1 Discuss the implications of the State hospital chaplain's statement.

2 Why do you think an individual might be unreceptive at one time and receptive at another? Discuss factors involved in receptivity.

3 Try to find someone who has had success in winning a neighbor. Ask some questions and see if you can uncover some principles.

4 Discuss the list of common mistakes committed by some beginning personal workers.

5 Can you add to the list of indicators of genuine interest? Talk over the list.

6 Do you know of any cases where interest was lost because of an approach that was too strong? What is the other extreme? Which extreme is worse?

7 Discuss Ellen White's statement about introducing arguments on the Sabbath question prematurely.

8 Talk over approaches to use when visiting media or literature interests. What would you say at the door? What are some specific things you would try to accomplish during the first visit?

9 Why do you think the Community Religious Survey is a widely successful method?

HANGING ON
THE SKIRTS
OF ZION

Inspiration describes the experience of professed Christians who neglect unselfish labor for others. "It is those who are not engaged in this unselfish labor who have a sickly experience, and become worn out with struggling, doubting, murmuring, sinning, and repenting, until they lose all sense as to what constitutes genuine religion. They feel that they cannot go back to the world, and so they hang on the skirts of Zion, having petty jealousies, envyings, disappointments, and remorse. They are full of fault finding, and feed upon the mistakes and errors of their brethren. They have only a hopeless, faithless, sunless experience in their religious life."—*Christian Service*, p. 107.

Reflection upon these words emphasizes the importance of Christians going to work for souls as soon as they are converted. Soul winning is a spiritual exercise that maintains spiritual health. The first-love experience is retained by leading others to a similar experience with Christ.

Our two focal points should be Christ and others. Satan is constantly seeking to make self the central concern in our lives. It is shocking to discover how much church activity is designed to minister to church members' needs rather than the needs of the world, when the very purpose of the church is service to others. We must never forget that "the church is God's appointed agency for the salvation of men. It was organized for service, and its mission is to carry the gospel to the world."—*Ibid.*, p. 15.

As we establish our priorities, we must determine whether the church exists for its members only or if its members exist to fulfill a mission to their community.

Ministry of the Laity

One writer says, "There will never be a widespread ministry of the laity until the church changes its direction, turns from its preoccupation with self to a concern for the world, offering itself as a servant."— Francis O. Ayres, *The Ministry of the Laity*, p. 132.

"If ... the whole church exists to serve the world and does not exist except as a servant, any restriction of the ministry to a small fraction of the church's membership becomes ridiculous."—*Ibid.*, p. 31.

In his book *A New Frontier—Every Believer a Minister*, Dr. Rex Edwards says, "The issue for the church today is not that here is a vast, untapped source of manpower that needs to be captured and put to work; the issue is that the church must come to know what is God's design for the laity in His eternal purpose. It is this that gives the direction to the layman's ministry. It is this that gives the layman motivation for his ministry. No program of promotion can take the place of this basic Biblical understanding."—Page 77.

Dr. Edwards correctly points out the importance of laymen understanding that they are indeed ministers with the privilege and responsibility of sharing the gospel. Bringing this awareness is, of course, basically a process of education.

The New Testament clearly teaches the priesthood of all believers. "But ye are a chosen generation, a royal priesthood, an holy nation, a peculiar people; that ye should shew forth the praises of him who hath called you out of darkness into his marvellous light" (1 Peter 2:9).

Perhaps the four most powerful factors motivating Christians to become involved in soul-winning activity are:

1. A deep love for Jesus Christ as Saviour and Lord.
2. Sharing Christ's burden for lost humanity.
3. Recognizing that the Lord considers each believer to be a minister.
4. Recognizing that there is a command to spread the gospel.

Curran L. Spottswood has well said, "There is no hope of winning this world to Christ through the efforts of professional missionaries and ministers only. It is far too big a job. The only hope in a day when the forces of darkness threaten to overwhelm us, is to mobilize the total manpower of the church—every pastor, every missionary, and also every lay man and woman must be Christ's ambassador, if we are even to begin to measure up to the fateful hour in which we live."

Speaking at a convocation sponsored by the Episcopal Theological Seminary, Amory Houghton, Jr., chairman of the board of the Corning Glass Works, referred to lay members as the "greatest untapped resource of the church." He chided the church for not using the laymen more effectively. He said, "Ask us to carry the gospel along with you. It will not embarrass us."

Clifford F. Hood, president of the U. S. Steel Corporation, speaking to the Episcopal Diocese of Pittsburgh, shared a similar sentiment when he said, "You can't leave the job to the clergy alone."

A commission on evangelism appointed by the Archbishops of Canterbury and York made this statement in its report: "The evangelism of England . . . is a work that cannot be done by the clergy alone; it can be done to a very small extent by the clergy at all. There can be no widespread evangelization of England unless the work is undertaken by the people of the church."

As soon as we recognize that every lay member, man or woman, is really a minister, the number of ministers in the average church suddenly jumps from one to a hundred or more, depending on the number of members. Recognition of the ministry of the laity is further reason for subdividing the church territory and giving a portion to each member or family, as discussed in the preceding chapter.

The mention of an assignment Sabbath when every family receives a mission field in which to work for the Lord, sometimes raises the question, "What about the members who are not fit to go out as representatives of the church?" Such members need gently to be helped by those who do have an experience with Jesus, to know Him meaningfully, also. But we also need to remember that fitness can only be maintained by unselfish service for others. That is why we are instructed that souls should be put to work as soon as they are converted. That is when each one should be assigned his post of duty. If we should fail to do this, the Lord forewarns us of the consequences. "Those who do not take up this work, those who act with the indifference that some have manifested, will soon lose their first love, and will begin to censure, criticize, and condemn their own brethren."—*Christian Service*, p. 115.

Clearly, this problem of unrepresentative members is a problem of our own making. "What can we expect but deterioration in religious life when the people listen to sermon after sermon and do not put the instruction into practice? The ability God has given, if not exercised, degenerates. More than this, when the churches are left to inactivity Satan sees to it that they

are employed. He occupies the field and engages the members in lines of work that absorb their energies, destroy spirituality, and cause them to fall as dead weights upon the church."—*Testimonies, vol. 6, p. 425.*
To keep this problem from developing, the church must:
1. Recognize and teach the obligation to witness.
2. Recognize and teach that every believer is a minister.
3. Make every church a training school.
4. Recognize the importance of small groups for missionary endeavor.
5. Recognize and apply the principle of assignment.
6. Encourage faithfulness in prayer and Bible study.

If we have members who are not spiritually qualified to be assigned a territory, major reasons are that either they never were thoroughly converted or that they were not assigned work as soon as they were converted. Consequently they have fallen into the spiritual maladies about which Inspiration has warned us, "So long as church members make no effort to give to others the help given them, great spiritual feebleness must result."—*Ibid., vol. 7, pp. 18, 19.*

Reclaiming Former Members

Another question that arises is, Shall we assign territories to backsliders? Former members have been reclaimed by giving them just such responsibility. Interestingly, we have a precedent from the experience of Ellen White. In describing a visit to a backslider, she says, "I visited with him, taking with me a few of my large books. I talked with him just as though he were with us. I talked of his responsibilities. I said, 'You have great responsibilities, my brother. Here are your neighbors all around you. You are accountable for every one of them. You have a knowledge of the truth, and if you love the truth, and stand in your integrity, you will win souls for Christ.' . . .

" 'Now,' I said, 'we are going to help you to begin to work for your neighbors. I want to make you a present of some books.' "

The account goes on to tell how this backslidden member loaned the books to his neighbors, and it ends with the words, "But suffice it to say, he took his position firmly for the truth. His whole family united with him, and they have been the means of saving other families."—*Evangelism*, pp. 451, 452.

Harley White had been the star Ingatherer in his church. A serious misunderstanding developed between him and another church member. This developed into a situation so serious that Harley asked to have his name removed from the church membership record. He still loved his Lord and his church, but his pride had been hurt. He didn't take up the ways of the world, but he avoided the church and its members.

When this church assigned territory a relatively new member was given the area where Harley lived. Harley's name was listed as a former member. The new member went to Harley's home for a friendship visit. As he told of his conversion experience and his joy in the Lord, it brought back to Harley memories of his own experience in past years. The new member talked of world conditions and fast-fulfilling prophecy. He spoke with enthusiasm of some of the current emphases in the church—spiritual gifts, Christ our righteousness, and Territorial Assignment—all manifestations of a deepening desire to see a finished work.

The new member described how Ingathering had brought increases in both baptisms and money since following the Territorial Assignment plan because the same person called at the same homes each year. Thus they were covering the same territory with other types of visits between Ingathering and were establishing meaningful friendships with the people.

Finally Harley's caller explained that every time there was an addition to church membership an existing territory was divided to provide territory for the new member.

The two men were drawn to each other during the visit. Harley was not able to resist when his visitor invited him to be his partner in his territory and give the benefit of his years of experience in the church. He made his decision that evening to come back to church and do his part in finishing the work. He responded on the basis of a call to service.

Seventh-day Adventists believe the time will come when members will go from home to home in the power of the Holy Spirit to give the loud cry. Some feel it will take persecution to stir the church to such action. Others believe it will result from a miraculous moving of the Holy Spirit. But the Holy Spirit is already moving. He is available now, awaiting our demand and reception. "God has done His part, and Christian activity is needed now. God calls for this."—*Christian Service*, p. 83.

God gives us a picture of the church as it is today, waiting for something to compel us to do what we know Christ expects us to do. "I was shown God's people waiting for some change to take place—a compelling power to take hold of them. But they will be disappointed, for they are wrong. They must act; they must take hold of the work themselves, and earnestly cry to God for a true knowledge of the work."—*Ibid.*, p. 82.

Let us not be found waiting for God when He is waiting for us. "The work of God in this earth can never be finished until the men and women comprising our church membership rally to the work, and unite their efforts with those of ministers and church officers."—

97

Ibid., p. 68. God has done His part. Now it is our turn to act. And when we do, God will give us power.

God has provided detailed instructions and is patiently waiting for us to follow them. "If the proper instruction were given, if the proper methods were followed, every church member would do his work as a member of the body."—*Evangelism*, p. 381.

Following the Lord's instructions will result in the majority of our members serving Him in harmony with their gifts and talents. Under those conditions we really sense our need of the Lord. We draw closer to Him and become more like Him. Instead of clinging to the skirts of Zion, we look to the church for fellowship and communion, and we reach out to the world for service.

Suggestions for Discussion

1 Consider the expenditures of time and money in your church. What is the balance between serving our own needs as church members and serving the needs of the unchurched community around us?

2 Discuss the four factors listed in this chapter that motivate Christians to become involved in soul-winning outreach. Can you add to them?

3 Discuss the two reasons given for there being unrepresentative members in some churches. Suggest other reasons.

4 Ellen White gave a former member books to share with his neighbors. In what other ways could this principle be applied?

5 Discuss the factors you believe caused Harley

White to return to the church?

6 Who would you like to have as a partner in your soul-winning projects? Give reasons for your choice.

7 What do you believe will stir the church to action?

8 Discuss the statement about proper instruction and methods.

9 In witnessing, are we waiting for God or is God waiting for us?

HALF
A
WITNESS

A meaningful witness is made up of two halves, each of which is as vital as the left and right wing of an airplane. These two halves are actions and words; the witness of the life and the witness by the word.

We have rare accounts of individuals who have come to know the Lord as a result of the words of someone who made no personal profession, or who was not living up to a profession of faith in Christ. An example of this is a man whose first contact with the Adventist message was through a backslidden member in a bar. Conversions resulting from such contacts are the exception rather than the rule. In such cases it is not "because of," but "in spite of."

Almost as rare are conversions resulting from the witness of Christians who quietly live "the life" but who never speak to others about their faith in the Lord Jesus Christ. This is not to minimize the importance of an exemplary Christian life. Without this as a foundation, words mean little or nothing. But the fact remains that in most cases it takes a combination of a consistant life and appropriate words of witness to lead another to conversion.

Letting Christ Live in You

There is no doubt that the apostle Paul lived an

exemplary life following his conversion experience. Undoubtedly, he made the finest tents available and was upright in all his business dealings. But it was because, in addition, he fervently shared the good news of salvation by grace through faith in Jesus Christ that he is remembered as one of the stalwarts of the Christian church.

Because Satan knows the converting power of a winning witness, he will try to weaken it by an inconsistent life or to silence our witness through fear or feelings of inadequacy. Inspiration indicates the importance of personal testimony in words that are penetratingly clear: "The two restored demoniacs were the first missionaries whom Christ sent to preach the gospel in the region of Decapolis. For a few moments only these men had been privileged to hear the teachings of Christ. Not one sermon from His lips had ever fallen upon their ears. They could not instruct the people as the disciples who had been daily with Christ were able to do. But they bore in their own persons the evidence that Jesus was the Messiah. They could tell what they knew; what they themselves had seen, and heard, and felt of the power of Christ. This is what everyone can do whose heart has been touched by the grace of God."—*The Desire of Ages*, p. 340.

Here were new converts. They could not give Bible studies yet, but they could testify to their own experience with Jesus Christ. *"This is what everyone can do whose heart has been touched by the grace of God."*

PRINCIPLE: *Every true Christian has a testimony to share.*

Every Christian can share experiences of answered prayer and tell of the power there is in claiming the promises of God. "We can tell how we have tested His promise, and found the promise true. We can bear witness to what we have known of the grace of Christ. This is the witness for which our Lord calls, and for want of which the world is perishing."—*Ibid.* No wonder Satan attempts to stifle our witness when its absence is causing many to perish.

The fact that living a model life alone is not enough is emphasized in this statement: "If professed Christians had engaged in this work from the time when their names were first placed on the church books, there would not now be such widespread unbelief, such depths of iniquity, such unparalleled wickedness, as is seen in the world at the present time. If every church member had sought to enlighten others, thousands upon thousands would today stand with God's commandment-keeping people."—*Testimonies,* vol. 6, p. 296.

Introducing Others to Christ

While we were holding meetings in a certain town, a prominent business family in the church gave us the name of their next-door neighbors and asked us to invite them to the meetings. Not only were they neighbors, but the husband was employed by the Adventist businessman. I thought, Why don't you invite them? The man works for you, you have lived next door to each other for years. If you can't get them to come to the meetings, there is little chance they will respond to the invitation of an absolute stranger. Nevertheless, I made the visit.

The people were friendly and invited me in. They had only good things to say about their Adventist neighbors. The witness of their lives had been consistent and positive. But when I invited them to attend the meetings, the answer in substance was, "You've come too late." They explained that a few weeks earlier an evangelical Christian had visited their home. At the close of the visit, after explaining the plan of salvation, he invited the family to kneel with him in prayer and commit their lives to Jesus. This man helped them to establish a personal relationship with Jesus Christ, and their appreciation was so great that when he invited them to attend his church, they agreed.

"We are so happy and active in our new church," the woman explained, "and it seems there's some activity every night of the week. So if we don't come to your meetings, you'll understand why, won't you?"

How wonderful it would have been if the Adventist neighbors had been the ones to kneel in the living room of that home and lead the family members to Jesus Christ. The Adventist family had provided the witness of a quiet Christian life. But their word of testimony had been missing. There was only half a witness.

In another city where we held meetings I was impressed by the happy disposition of one of our members. This man had volunteered to help cut down expenses by providing the janitorial service at the auditorium where our crusade was being held. He brought a number of friends to the meetings, some of whom were baptized. But the thing that impressed me most was his consistently happy nature. I asked him about it one day. He explained that he was a new member, happy in his new-found faith. It had begun when he and his wife started watching the *It Is Written* telecast. A young couple from the local church had visited them and had made a good impression. Later they brought the pastor, and the happy experience climaxed in the baptism of this man and his wife.

He then told me how they had made a missionary journey back to the State where they had lived most of their lives. They had gone from farm to farm visiting their old neighbors and telling them of their joy in the Lord.

As they came to the farm next to where they had lived for so many years, the man said to his wife, "We won't have to tell them about our new faith; they already know. They were Seventh-day Adventists all through the years that we lived next to them. The husband was a church elder, and yet they never spoke to us of their faith."

As they visited with their former next-door neighbors, the new member chided good-naturedly, "Why was it that we had to move to another State to learn these wonderful things that you knew all the time? Why didn't you tell us?"

Embarrassed, the church elder said, "There were many times through the years when we wanted to say something, but we were afraid it might interfere with our friendship."

"Oh, but just think," said the new member, embracing the longtime neighbor, "now we can be friends for all eternity!"

If we really know Jesus as a personal friend it should not be difficult for us to introduce Him to our earthly friends. *Witnessing for Christ* is our denominational witnessing manual written expressly for the purpose of teaching us how to lead a soul to Jesus. For people who find it difficult to memorize the outline of a study on the plan of salvation, there are little booklets available outlining the simple steps. One of the best is called, *Opinion, Please.** This booklet is profusely illustrated and is designed so that the witness and the prospect can

---

* *Opinion, Please* booklets may be ordered from the General Conference Department of Lay Activities.

read it together. This procedure works remarkably well.

An opening for such a presentation can often be made by weaving into your conversation the question, "In your opinion, how does one become a Christian?"

You will get answers such as By being born into a Christian family, By trying to live a good life, By living according to the golden rule, By keeping the Ten Commandments, By baptism. All these answers indicate a faulty understanding of the plan of salvation and a dependence upon works rather than grace for salvation. Even some who give a Biblically correct answer may know the theory but may not have had the actual experience of personally receiving Jesus Christ.

Where there is indication of a faulty understanding of the plan of salvation, you can proceed by asking, "Could we take a few minutes and look at seven or eight verses that explain how one becomes a Christian?" If there is an affirmative answer you can proceed with the gospel presentation as found in the *Opinion, Please* booklet.

This simple study is built around the following eight texts: 1 John 4:8; Romans 3:23; John 3:16; Romans 6:23; Ephesians 2:8, 9; 1 John 5:11-13; Romans 2:4; and Revelation 3:20.

The booklet uses the illustration of a couple who can believe in each other, know each other, and love each other without being married. A couple become husband and wife when they exchange marriage vows. Likewise you can believe in the existence of Christ without being a Christian. You become a Christian when you love Christ enough to receive Him as your Saviour and Lord.

This prayer of commitment is printed in the booklet:

"Dear God, I invite You to take control of my life. I want Jesus to come into my heart. I want Him to be my Saviour and my Lord. Please forgive my sins. And thank You for giving me eternal life in Jesus. Help me to follow and obey Him. In Jesus' name, amen.''

If your prospect agrees after reading this prayer that it expresses the desire of his heart, you can pray the prayer together, or you can invite him to express these thoughts in his own words in a simple prayer to God.

Such a decision can mark the turning point in a human life. The way must be prepared for this moment of decision by laying a foundation of friendship, and there must be faithful follow-up to guarantee a growing spiritual experience.

Let me emphasize that it is not necessary to memorize a lengthy presentation. You can read everything, word for word, with your prospect from *Opinion, Please*. In addition to this, virtually all of our newer Bible lessons series have the gospel presentation as one of their early lessons. The timing of this presentation will vary. In most cases it will come after three or four Christ-centered Bible studies that give an opportunity to win the confidence of your prospect. On rare occasions you will find someone who has been prepared by the Holy Spirit for the moment of surrender. In such cases you can give the gospel presentation on your first visit. But this will certainly be the exception rather than the rule.

Experiencing the thrill of helping a fellow human being establish a meaningful relationship with Jesus Christ can be the greatest joy of your life. There are undoubtedly some laymen in your church who have learned how to do this. They should be encouraged to take someone else with them as they visit so that others may learn from their example.

"There are many who want to know what they must do to be saved. They want a plain and clear explanation of the steps requisite in conversion, and . . . [workers should] especially make plain the way that sinners may come to Christ and be saved."—*Evangelism*, p. 188.

A simple portrayal of how to establish a personal and meaningful relationship with Jesus is the greatest need of many backsliders. Many have had a theoretical knowledge but have never had a personal experience with the Lord.

Christ is a fact of conscience, especially in "Christian" lands. There are many who feel their need of receiving Him, and they will respond positively when given the opportunity. These prospects are scattered in every neighborhood. "My brethren and sisters, there are souls in your neighborhood who, if they were judiciously labored for, would be converted."—*Ibid.*, p. 114. Some of these prospects find us by happening to tune in to an Adventist radio or television program or through a chance meeting with a Seventh-day Adventist. Some of them find themselves living next door to an Adventist family. But we cannot expect Providence to move all the prospects next door. Many will be found only if we search for them. No wonder, then, that Inspiration says, "This house-to-house labor, searching for souls, hunting for the lost sheep, is the most essential work that can be done."—*Ibid.*, p. 431.

Let us ask the Lord to help us to put together the two halves of a winning witness—the testimony of a consistent Christian life plus the verbal testimony of our faith in Christ.

Suggestions for Discussion

1 What are some ways by which Satan tries to weaken our witness?

2 Can everyone who has experienced conversion do what the healed demoniacs did?

3 Discuss what the Spirit of Prophecy has to say

about the relationship between the testimony of Christians and world conditions.

4 Should we put more emphasis on teaching how to introduce a person to Jesus?

5 Jesus told the healed demoniac to go to his acquaintances and share his testimony. Does this imply that it was not entirely a spontaneous, automatic action? Did the new convert need a little guidance as to what he should do?

6 What testimony does one have who was reared in a Christian home and has never known anything besides a Christian environment?

7 Discuss things to keep in mind when visiting a former member.

HOW TO
GET
DECISIONS

The gospel is intended to be good news, but it can be that only when we follow divine instruction and introduce the soul to Christ before we present the individual with Christ's testing teachings. A person must have the presence and power of Christ in his life if he is to make right decisions.

A decision is a resolute determination to act based on choice. Intelligent choices require:

1. As adequate and accurate information as is possible.

2. Confidence in the source of the information.

3. A clear mind.

4. Motivation.

In the case of the Christian, every decision should be influenced by a determination to do what is right in the sight of God. Such decisions can be made only by the power of the Holy Spirit.

In helping people to make right decisions it is important to know something about motivation. A recent survey showed the four strongest motivators to be (1) self-preservation, (2) security, (3) happiness, and (4) acquisition (gaining something you do not have or preventing the loss of something you do have). Keep these principles in mind as we think about getting decisions for Christ and His teachings. Bear in mind that we must always begin with a person where he is and lead him from that point to where God wants him to be.

"Christ drew the hearts of His hearers to Him by the manifestation of His love, and then, little by little, as they were able to bear it, He unfolded to them the great truths of the kingdom. We also must learn to adapt our labors to the condition of the people—to meet men where they are. While the claims of the law of God are to be presented to the world, we should never forget that love—the love of Christ—is the only power that can soften the heart and lead to obedience."—*Evangelism,* pp. 484, 485.

The doctrines of the Bible are like massive blocks of stone that are square, and true, and enduring, each fitting perfectly with the others in a beautiful, harmonious structure. But, depending upon how we present these doctrines, we build for our prospect a wall or a stairway. First, let us illustrate the former.

We present a Bible study on the second coming of Christ. To us who believe, this is indeed good news. Christ is coming again to bring to an end the reign of sin and to take us to be with Him in the heavenly mansions. But many who do not know the Lord are filled with fear at the thought of His coming, and judgment, and the end of the world. To them it conjures up scenes of fiery destruction. Everything that means security to them will be destroyed. They have no assurance of going to heaven. They perhaps have heard that heaven and earth will be destroyed. Where does that leave them? To the one who is unprepared, this is bad news.

Consider the subject of the Sabbath. This is a theme we greatly enjoy because we love the Lord of the Sabbath. But we're dealing with a person who does not know Him. He works on Saturday. As a matter of fact, it is his busiest day. Now we are telling him that to work on this day is sin. It will bring death.

The world is going to be destroyed, and he is doomed

to death because he works on the Sabbath, as well as committing other sins. This indeed is bad news.

We come back for a study on tithing. We appreciate the privilege of partnership with the Lord, but our prospect doesn't know the Lord, and what is good news to us is bad news to him. The world is going to be destroyed, he can't work on the Sabbath, which is his best day of business, and the church is going to take 10 percent of his money, although he's having difficulty paying his bills. What he is hearing is to him bad news.

Then comes the study on healthful living. We Adventists appreciate a life style that adds more than six years to the life of the average SDA, but pork is our prospect's favorite food. So he doesn't know the Lord, the world is going to be destroyed, he must give up his best day of business, the church is going to take 10 percent of his money, and now he is to be deprived of his favorite food! This is very bad news.

Finally, we come to our last study. (Remember, this is an illustration. We are not attempting to set forth the ideal order of subjects; no one would think of presenting one testing truth after another as we have done in this illustration. The final study is an appeal for decision and church membership. We are hoping for an affirmative decision. What we fail to recognize is that, because of some neglect and failure on our part, a negative decision was made by our prospect after each study without our even calling for it. What we have unwittingly done is build a seemingly insurmoutable wall in front of him composed of the very truths we trusted would lead him to Christ and the church.

The wall is so high that the prospect cannot see the Christ of the cross on the other side. We expect him to get over this wall in one gigantic leap, but to him it is an utter impossibility. When we ask for his decision, he says, "This religion might be all right for you, but I could never live up to it. I could never meet all those requirements."

When we hear this, we are bitterly disappointed. We have conscientiously invested our time in giving these Bible studies, hoping for a baptism to result, but our prospect gives an emphatic *No.* How could we have done it differently? The key is found in the following words: "The very first and most important thing is to melt and subdue the soul by presenting our Lord Jesus Christ as the sin-pardoning Saviour."—*Testimonies,* vol.6, pp. 53, 54. "Of all professing Christians, Seventh-day Adventists should be foremost in uplifting Christ before the world."—*Gospel Workers,* p. 156.

> *PRINCIPLE: Introduce the person to Christ before presenting testing truths.*

Presenting Christ First

Let us demonstrate a better approach. The very first thing we do is to bring the prospect to a personal relationship with Jesus Christ. We do this by giving our own personal testimony, by Christ-centered Bible studies on the plan of salvation, and by a simple gospel presentation.

As you read on, watch for the application of the following principles:

1. As you approach each study decide on the main point you want to get across to your prospect.

2. Have clearly in mind the decision you're going to ask for at the conclusion of the study.

3. Point out the happiness and benefits that will result from making this decision.

4. Encourage the prospect to incorporate immediately into his way of life the truths he learns from the Bible.

5. Remember that once a person agrees to a minor action, he is much more likely to agree to a major one.

6. Get the prospect to express his decision in words. Expression deepens impression.

7. Apply the principle of progressive decisions. The longest journey is made by taking one step at a time.

8. Approach a prospect with enthusiasm, cheerfulness, optimism, confidence, and expectation.

Let us now return to the doctrines we previously discussed that made for our prospect practically insurmountable problems, but now we have led him to Jesus Christ as Saviour and Lord. Now as we present the second coming of Christ, we are talking to one who knows the Christ of the coming, the Saviour who loved Him enough to bear the agonies of Calvary. The news that this same Jesus is coming again is now good news. The prospect ponders the thrill that will be his to look into the face of the One who took his place on the cross. Following the study, we ask some simple questions to be sure the presentation was clear. We call for a decision. "Is it clear to you now that Jesus will come again? Do you find a desire in your heart to be ready to meet Him in peace?"

> PRINCIPLE: Progressive decisions. Ask for a decision as each subject is presented.

Think, now, of the study about the Sabbath. Our prospect has learned to know and love the Lord of the Sabbath. We explain that from the beginning of the

113

world, the Lord set apart a special day that would be a foretaste of heaven. Through His miraculous power, He guarantees that in six days His followers will be able to provide for all their needs and to find bread for the seventh day.

We point out that the Sabbath is a wonderful day in which we can lay aside all earthly cares, a day when the family can be together with the Lord in worship and in service. It is one thing when people are thrown together because they work together each day. But when they choose to spend their day off together, that proves there is a special relationship between them. God is actually asking us to spend our day off with Him. This thought pleases our prospect very much. Again we ask questions to be sure he understands. Then we invite a decision. "Now that you understand the love that prompted God to provide the Sabbath, do you want to make plans to reserve this holy time to be spent with Him?" And this beautiful teaching becomes another block, not in a wall, but in steps that lead steadily upward, and our prospect takes another step by making one more decision in favor of the teachings of Jesus Christ.

Think of the study on tithing. Our prospect is a businessman, and as we talk of partnership with God, he realizes that a partnership is usually a 50-50 proposition. We explain that God is offering us a partnership on a 90-10 basis. He allows us to keep 90 percent. He requires only a minimum amount to make the partnership valid. He promises us health and sunshine, food and friends, and all He asks is that we respect and return 10 percent as His portion. Our prospect is so overwhelmed that he responds, "Why certainly, I'll return His 10 percent. In addition to that, I'll give Him at least another 10 percent as offerings to be used for projects that are close to His heart." Our prospect has taken another step walking in the light.

When we come to the study on healthful living, I mention that there are two women who have expressed a concern about what I eat. One is my mother, the other is my wife. Why should they be concerned about what I eat? Because they love me. They want me to live and enjoy good health. What, then, do I conclude as I study the Bible and learn that God also is concerned about what I take into my body? That He loves me too; He wants me to enjoy life and health. It is only for our own good that He has given us these health counsels.

Even before we finish our study, our prospect indicates that he understands and accepts. He has placed his feet on yet another steppingstone.

Finally, we come to the last study and the appeal for decision and church membership. Because our prospect has been walking in the light step by step, this decision represents only one more step in the direction he has already been going. Already he has learned the priceless principle, "I can do all things through Christ which strengtheneth me" (Phil. 4:13). He is not trusting in his own ability to obey but in the Christ whom he invited into his heart at the very beginning of the studies. And now, in one final act of surrender, he determines to go all the way with Christ. He is actually eager to be baptized and to become a part of the church. He wants to be of service. He wants to share with others the truths that have brought about such a beautiful change in his life. He wants to follow Jesus in fishing for men. He has caught the thrill of the momentum of a movement, and he wants to join his voice to the chorus that gives the invitation, "Come." He has heard good news and he wants to share it.

If you do not feel ready at this point to tackle the area of getting decisions, remember, you do have options. Invite your prospect to the pastor's Bible class and let him get the decision. Another excellent way is to take your prospect with you to a series of evangelistic meetings.

The business of getting decisions is perhaps the most challenging as well as the most rewarding part of personal work. It is the area in which most laymen feel a desperate need for help. For that reason the remainder of this chapter will offer practical suggestions on the deeper aspects of decision getting. If you find yourself not ready for it yet, go on to the next chapter and reserve this portion for some later time. On the other hand, if you are curious to understand some of the principles governing the human decision-making process, read on.

Mind, Will, and Heart

The decision process involves the mind, the will, and the heart. A positive response in each of these areas depends upon one's personal relationship with Jesus Christ.

The terms mind and heart are not ordinarily used in the Bible in the sense in which we employ them today. In Scriptures they are frequently general terms comprising more than we mean by them. In modern terms the mind has to do with gathering and evaluating information, and we here use the word in this sense.

Regarding the will, Ellen White says, "The will is the governing power in the nature of man, bringing all the other faculties under its sway. . . . It is the deciding power which works in the children of men unto obedience to God or unto disobedience."—*Testimonies*, vol. 5, p. 513. "You cannot control your impulses, your emotions, as you may desire; but you can control the will, and you can make an entire change in your life. By yielding up your will to Christ, your life will be hid with Christ in God. . . . You will have strength from God that will hold you fast to His strength."—*Ibid.*,

p. 514. "Everything depends on the right action of the will."—*The Ministry of Healing*, p. 176.

We must have the power of Christ to do what we will to do (see Rom. 7:18). "Our will is not to be forced into cooperation with divine agencies."—*Thoughts From the Mount of Blessing*, p. 142. "If you are 'willing to be made willing,' God will accomplish the work for you."—*Ibid*.

Experience confirms the observation that in any battle involving the will, the intellect, and the emotions, in the unconverted person the emotions usually win. Let's give careful thought then to the following statements about the heart in relation to decision. (We recognize that Ellen White has more than emotions in mind when she refers to heart in the sense used here. But emotions are clearly included.)

"Love—the love of Christ—is the only power that can soften the heart and lead to obedience."—*Evangelism*, p. 485. "Your success will not depend so much upon your knowledge and accomplishments, as upon your ability to find your way to the heart."—*Ibid.*, p. 483. "The true heart-expression of Christlike sympathy, given in simplicity, has power to open the door of hearts that need the simple, delicate touch of the Spirit of Christ."—*Ibid*.

The angels of heaven draw close to aid us when we are asking for a decision. The wisdom of the angels is at our disposal.

A factor that will help us greatly in our efforts to win souls to Christ is our capacity to love people. Think about these two statements:

"Kindly words simply spoken, little attentions simply bestowed, will sweep away the clouds of temptation and doubt that gather over the soul."—*Ibid*.

"By being social and coming close to the people, you may turn the current of their thoughts more readily than by the most able discourse."—*Ibid.*

Decision Signals

An intuition for the correct time to call for a decision is something that is gained by experience. We learn to become alert to indications that a prospect is considering decision. Here is a list of what we might call decision signals:

1. "I wish my husband were more agreeable to my becoming an Adventist."

2. "I wonder if I would lose my job if I asked for Sabbath off."

3. "I have some tithe to give you."

4. "Would I have to quit going to shows?"

5. "What would I do all day Saturday?"

Decision-getting Methods

Appeals should be specific. Here are three steps that have been used successfully in gaining decisions:

1. "You believe that what you have learned in our studies as the truth of God, don't you?"

2. "You do plan to follow Jesus all the way, don't you?"

3. "Let's kneel together and ask God for grace to do it now."

The devil has "iron bands" that he uses to hinder people from making their decision.

"Many are convinced that we have the truth, and yet they are held as with iron bands; they dare not risk the consequences of taking their position on the side of truth. . . . Just at this critical period Satan throws the strongest bands around these souls."—*Testimonies,* vol. 1, p. 646.

We might classify these "bands" as economic,

social, and spiritual. Let's think about these categories.
1. Economic:
   a. Fear of losing employment.
   b. Lacking faith to tithe.
2. Social:
   a. Opposition from a loved one.
   b. Fear of ridicule.
   c. Fear of dividing the family.
   d. Concern for what friends will say.
3. Spiritual:
   a. Sentimental ties to family church.
   b. Opposition from the pastor.
   c. Prestige of belonging to popular church.

We must determine what the obstacle is before we can clear it away. We can uncover the problems by asking questions such as:
1. "Is everything clear to you?"
2. "Do you see any problems if you should move forward?"
3. "What do you have in mind?"
4. "When you think about being baptized what comes into your mind?"

There are ways in which we can help people to overcome obstacles to decision:
1. Pray with and for the individual. Teach him to pray.
2. Lead the prospect to claim the promises of God. Help him in searching for these promises in the Bible and the Spirit of Prophecy. Your own experience will be enriched by searching out the promises of God. There is one for every need. When a prospect has a problem it is effective to say, "Yes, you have a problem, but God has a solution. I have been praying about your problem, and God impressed me to read this chapter in the Bible. I read the entire chapter, and when I came to this verse I wondered if it would not help in solving your problem."

A WALL OR STEPS?
A Wrong Way

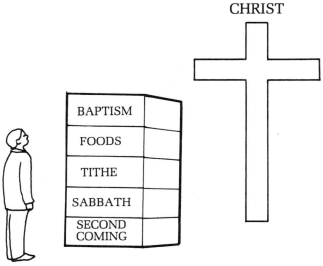

CHRIST

BAPTISM

FOODS

TITHE

SABBATH

SECOND COMING

A Right Way

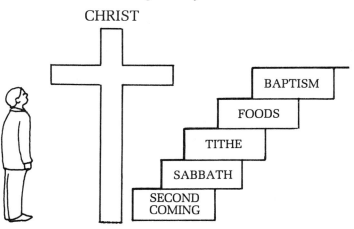

CHRIST

BAPTISM

FOODS

TITHE

SABBATH

SECOND COMING

Ask your prospect to read the appropriate verse, and usually he will say, "I see the answer to my problem is right here."

3. Encourage the prospect to exercise the faith he has. Faith increases with exercise. It comes by "hearing"—studying and following—the Word of God. Encourage the prospect to spend time daily in Bible study.

4. Full surrender clears away all difficulties. "As souls give themselves to the Lord Jesus, making an entire surrender, they will understand the doctrine."—*Evangelism*, p. 465.

Memorize the following quotation; you will find many opportunities to use it in working with others: "Our heavenly Father has a thousand ways to provide for us of which we know nothing. Those who accept the one principle of making the service of God supreme, will find perplexities vanish and a plain path before their feet."—*The Ministry of Healing*, p. 481.

Perhaps the most basic principle of all in gaining decisions is simply to remember to ask for one. This is so elementary it is sometimes taken for granted and neglected. You are not likely to get a decision if you don't ask for it.

Ask for a favorable decision by offering a choice. For example, "We are planning baptisms on June 1 and 15. Which date would be best for you?"

"Would you prefer to go into the water first, or do you prefer to have your children baptized first?"

You can also get a decision by the use of an indirect question: "Would you write your name on this piece of paper the way you would like to have it on your baptismal certificate?"

"Is there a special song you would like immediately preceding your baptism?"

Let us review the important points of this chapter:

1. Begin at the first study to ask for progressive decisions.

2. Encourage your prospect not only to give mental assent to truth but to put into practice each new duty as it unfolds. Walking in the light is a prerequisite for more light.

3. Beginning with the first few studies. Invite your prospect to the services and activities of the church. Combine such invitations with Sabbath dinner invitations.

4. Help your prospect to establish new friendships with church members.

5. Keep in mind that it is the goodness of God that leads to repentance (Rom. 2:4).

6. Do not base appeals for decision on abstract doctrines but on a practical application of the teachings of Christ to everyday life.

Gaining decisions is a matter of helping fellow human beings to get personally acquainted with Jesus Christ as Saviour and Lord. Our work is beautifully portrayed in these words: "With one hand the workers would take hold of Christ, while with the other they would grasp sinners and draw them to the Saviour."—*Evangelism*, p. 293.

The greatest of all appeals is the appeal of the cross. "Christ crucified—talk it, pray it, sing it, and it will break and win hearts."—*Testimonies*, vol. 6, p. 67.

Suggestions for Discussion

1 Can we present Christ without presenting doctrine?

2 Can we present doctrine without presenting Christ?

3 Can we present information about Christ and His teachings without helping a person to establish a meaningful personal relationship with Him?

4 Discuss the principle of progressive decisions.

5 Discuss the role of the will, the intellect, and the emotions in relation to decision and in light of the statement that "everything depends on the right action of the will."

6 How important do you consider social aspects of decision making to be? What can the church do in this area to create a favorable climate?

7 Discuss ways of helping people to break through the economic, social, and spiritual "bands" that hinder their decision.

8 One of the best indicators that a favorable decision is pending is action on the part of the prospect stemming from what has been learned in the studies. What are some of the actions or changes in life style to look for?

ALTERNATIVES TO GUILT

More than one lay leader has struggled with the question, How can we encourage greater participation in personal evangelism without increasing the guilt level of church members? For the most part our church members are sincere, dedicated, and conscientious. Why, then, does the problem of guilt arise?

Feelings of guilt and frustration result when members are made to feel obligated to perform duties for which they do not feel suited or qualified.

The Problem of Fear

Millie MacIntosh actually experienced extreme nausea every time her church scheduled a literature visitation day. Usually there would be a sermon about the duty of the members to knock on doors and distribute literature. Millie wanted to do her part, but she found it extremely difficult to meet strangers. The combination of frustration and guilt actually made her temporarily ill. A friend in the church became aware of the problem and invited Millie to be her silent partner. Even thinking of this made Millie have feelings of nausea before the first visitation day. But not again. The first afternoon with someone who was experienced and confident dispelled all her fears. She still did not feel she could do it, but she actually looked forward to going along as a silent partner. After doing this several times, Millie finally gained sufficient confidence to take the lead in visitation. Eventually, she actually enjoyed it. And she found great personal satisfaction in having overcome her fears and guilt.

Jesus sent His disciples in teams of two (Mark 6:7). He also gave them the privilege of three and one-half years of close association with Him. Day after day they had opportunity to watch His actions and listen to His words as He ministered to people. This is what we call on-the-job training. Every Adventist church should be a training school.

Churches as Training Schools

"Many would be willing to work if they were taught how to begin. They need to be instructed and encouraged. Every church should be a training school for Christian workers. . . . There should not only be teaching, but actual work under experienced instructors. Let the teachers lead the way in working among the people, and others, uniting with them, will learn from their example."—*Christian Service*, p. 59.

> PRINCIPLE: *Every church should be a practical training school; there should be on-the-job training.*

No wonder many church members are plagued by fear and guilt if they are assigned responsibility without being trained to fulfill the responsibility! The problems of guilt and fear could be virtually eradicated if provision were made for on-the-job training. Laymen who have had experience and a degree of success in personal evangelism should make themselves available to accompany new or inexperienced members in visitation until they also gain experience and confidence. This is the principle of discipling that enables the worker force in the church to keep multiplying.

Remember, Jesus devoted three and one-half years to the training of twelve disciples. Eleven of the twelve became successful and in turn trained others, who trained still others, so that the working force of personal evangelists was multiplied greatly. Our denominational witnessing manual, *Witnessing for Christ*, available at your ABC, describes how this same principle can be employed in the church today.

Here are three constructive measures that will help to avoid increasing the level of guilt experienced by church members.

1. Recognize the diversity of talents and spiritual gifts and do not try to put everyone in the same mold.

2. Provide on-the-job training for whatever time is necessary to build confidence.

3. Encourage members to work in teams of two, one of whom is experienced.

If proper training and encouragement is provided, every member can become a soul winner, working in his own armor and using his gifts to the glory of God.

PRINCIPLE: *"Every Christian is to be a missionary."*—Christian Service, p. 22

"I have emphasized one truth in my church over and over. I have repeated it until my people have finally come to believe it. . . . They actually believe they should win souls; therefore, they do."—Gene Edwards, *How to Have a Soul-Winning Church*, p. 57.

There is no substitute for personal labor. "By personal labor reach those around you. Become acquainted with them. Preaching will not do the work that needs to be done. Angels of God attend you to the dwellings of those you visit. This work cannot be done by proxy. Money lent or given will not accomplish it. Sermons will not do it. By visiting the people, talking, praying, sympathizing with them, you will win hearts."—*Christian Service*, pp. 117, 118.

Too many Christians limit their participation to God's cause to going to church and giving to missions. The Lord expects more than this. The Bible does not diminish guilt resulting from unfaithfulness to duty. "When I say unto the wicked, O wicked man, thou shalt surely die; if thou dost not speak to warn the wicked from his way, that wicked man shall die in his iniquity; but his blood will I require at thine hand" (Eze. 33:8).

Where the Lord has given responsibility there is inevitably guilt to be charged against the one who neglects his duty. "The Lord holds the church responsible for the souls of those whom they might be the means of saving."—*Ibid.*, p. 13.

Guilt causes pain, and pain is sometimes a blessing in disguise. It informs that something is wrong. Something is indeed wrong if a Christian feels no compulsion to share his joy in the Lord with others.

"You are guilty before God if you do not make every effort possible to dispense this living water to others."—*Ibid.*, p. 12.

Physical pain is usually a symptom of an organic problem. The pain of guilt is probably a symptom of a spiritual problem. When there are symptoms of disease we endanger ourselves when we avoid diagnosis. Ceasing to face up to our duty is a dangerous and self-deceiving way of dealing with the problem of guilt. Guilt is a symptom. The problem might be a lack of training; it might also be disobedience to the gospel commission.

Consider the following alternatives to guilt:

1. Providing training classes to equip the church for service.

2. On-the-job training.

3. Working in teams of two—teaming up weaker members with stronger ones.

4. Multiplying workers through discipling.

5. Accepting willingly God-given responsibility.

The enemy of souls will do everything in his power to keep the people of God from involvement in one-to-one personal work. Other programs gain enthusiastic reception, but not this one. Why not?

One writer suggests, "The answer is not far to find. This Program is altogether *divine*, and so it is impossible to carry it out except by *divine power*. . . . It is nothing short of complete death to all we are and have. . . .

"This is why we are so busy making and following human programs. For to follow the divine Program requires us to pay a price that even many leaders in the Church seem unwilling to pay. And so we busy ourselves with programs of civilization, education, social service, and a dozen other by-products of evangelism, and let straight-out personal work for lost souls go, never seeming to realize that when we stop evangelizing the by-products will disappear in spite of all we can do to continue them."—J. E. Conant, *Every Member Evangelism*, pp. 120, 121.

The same author shares this illustration: "A man had given himself to Christ for Africa. A friend said to him, 'Isn't it dangerous to go so far away from civilization, where you will have no help and no medicine in

sickness? Aren't you afraid you'll die?'
" 'I died when I decided to go,' said the missionary."
This brings us directly to the crux of the whole
matter. It is self versus the command of God. But self is
too cunning to admit such a simple analysis, so we
rationalize that we do not have the necessary gifts, that
this is not our talent, and so forth.

Dawson Trotman, founder of The Navigators, a
well-known evangelical group that emphasizes personal evangelism, admitted after twenty-nine years of
leadership in personal work, "It still frightens me to talk
to a man about his need of salvation." Almost all
personal workers will make a similar admission. It is
hard because the devil doesn't want us to do it.

Meeting Felt Human Needs

Christ set us an example in working for others.
"Christ's method alone will give true sucess in reaching
the people. The Saviour mingled with men as one who
desired their good. He showed His sympathy for them,
ministered to their needs, and won their confidence.
Then, He bade them, 'Follow Me.' "—*Welfare Ministry*,
p. 60.

The basic human needs of the lonely, discouraged,
and troubled are the same today as when Jesus lived on
earth. Doors and hearts will open to us as we go forth to
meet these needs in the spirit of the Master.

"My brethren and sisters, visit those who live near
you, and by sympathy and kindness seek to reach their
hearts. Be sure to work in a way that will remove
prejudice instead of creating it. And remember that
those who know the truth for this time, and yet confine
their efforts to their own churches, refusing to work for
their unconverted neighbors, will be called to account
for unfulfilled duties."—*Christian Service*, p. 115.

HTHYCG-9

> PRINCIPLE: Remove prejudice,
> don't create it.

As we take time to get acquainted with our neighbors, we will discover many natural openings. We can take an interest in the little children as Jesus did. We will discover sadness and loneliness and, in the spirit of the Saviour, we will be able to bring comfort. "Our Saviour went from house to house. . . . He took the little children in His arms. . . . With unfailing tenderness and gentleness, He met every form of human woe and affliction."—*Ibid.*, p. 114. You will find opportunity to exercise your spiritual gifts in your neighborhood, and by following the example of Jesus in service to others, you will find an alternative to guilt.

Suggestions for Discussion

1 Discuss the importance of instructors leading the way in working with nonchurch people— in other words, on-the-job training.

2 Discuss the three suggestions for lessening the problem of guilt.

3 What are some indications of our attempts to do our soul winning by proxy?

4 Discuss the five suggested alternatives to guilt. Do you have any to add to the list?

5 In what ways do you think "self" enters into our fears of participating in personal evangelism?

6 Discuss removing the prejudice of people we

contact versus creating prejudice.

7 What significance do you see in testimonies
from veteran personal workers indicating
they still battle fear and reluctance to talk to
others about Christ and spiritual matters?

8 List some of the natural ways of witnessing you
can think of.

9 What is the greatest fear you have about sharing
your faith with strangers? What can you do
to overcome this fear? Are you concerned
about what they will think of Christ or about
what they will think of you? Can you think
of one supreme reason why you should not
be afraid?

TELL
IT
EVERYWHERE

The 4-year old daughter of a pastor was pretending she was a preacher like her daddy. She knew a preacher needs a pulpit, and, of course, there wasn't a pulpit in the living room, so she used a chair and a little imagination.

Finding a congregation was a little more difficult. At first she tried to make one out of her brother and sister, but they were both older and wouldn't sit still and be quiet the way a congregation should. Finally she gave up on them and found a new congregation in her toy box—a congregation of dolls and teddy bears. They stayed in their places and remained perfectly still and very quiet.

Just about the time her mommy looked in on the scene, the little preacher girl left her pulpit, walked down into the congregation, and, standing in front of one of the teddy bears, said to him, "I'm going to baptize you today."

Her mother thought, This is a good opportunity for me to teach my little girl something of the importance of baptism. She walked into the room, put her arm around her little one, and said, "Honey, do you realize that before a person is baptized, he must give his heart to Jesus? He must know something of the teachings of Jesus, and many times there are habits that must be laid aside in preparation for baptism."

The little girl listened patiently. Then it was her turn to talk: "Mommy, he has given his heart to Jesus. I've given him Bible studies; I've given him books to read. He's quit smoking, and I'm going to baptize him!"

The mother was quite pleased to see how much her daughter knew about baptism, but she decided to keep an eye and an ear on what was transpiring in the living room as the little preacher girl made preparation for the baptism. She was relieved that her daughter was going to use her imagination as far as the water was concerned.

Finally, the 4-year-old was ready to proceed with the baptism. Holding the teddy bear in one hand she raised the other in benediction as she had seen her daddy do. Then, she tried to remember what her daddy said when he baptized someone. Thinking hard she remembered part of it, and maybe part of what she had learned as a memory verse in Sabbath School. Then her mother heard her say, as she baptized the teddy bear, "In that you've done what you could, I now baptize you."

She Did What She Could

It appears that Mark 14:8, the words that Jesus spoke concerning the woman of the long ago who anointed Him with expensive ointment, was the basis of her baptismal formula. Others criticized the woman for her act and called it extravagant, but Jesus defended her. He said, "Let her alone; why trouble ye her? she hath wrought a good work on me. For ye have the poor with you always, and whensoever ye will ye may do them good: but me ye have not always. She hath done what she could: she is come aforehand to anoint my body to the burying" (vs. 6-8).

The ninth verse of this chapter was indelibly impressed upon my mind one night at the close of an evangelistic sermon when a fiery-eyed visitor challenged me with the question, "Do you preach everything that Jesus said should be preached?"

He had his Bible open to this verse and, shaking a finger in my face, read, "Verily I say unto you, Wheresoever this gospel shall be preached throughout the whole world, this also that she hath done shall be spoken of for a memorial of her."

"Do you do it?" he demanded. "Jesus said to tell it everywhere—wherever the gospel is preached."

I went home and restudied the chapter, for I must admit I know of no other passage where Jesus used such strong emphasis. Wherever this gospel shall be preached throughout the whole world, He said, "this also that she hath done shall be spoken of for a memorial of her." What was there about this episode that caused Jesus to give it such emphasis? I believe He wanted us to think about the potential of every believer "doing what he could."

There are at least four things in the experience of this woman that have parallels in your experience and mine.

She was probably an average person. We do not read of any special gifts or talents she possessed. Those of us who feel that we are average gain courage from her experience to believe that we, too, might win words of commendation from our Lord if we will do what is in our power to do to share His love with others.

She loved Jesus very much. This is something else we, it is hoped, have in common with this woman.

She put her love into action even at the risk of becoming the object of criticism. That love motivated her so strongly that she had to do something to declare it for her Lord.

She had a sense of urgency. Not only did she have good intentions, she carried them out before it was too late.

She lived just before Jesus left this earth to return to

heaven. We live just before Jesus will leave heaven to return to this earth. She lived on one edge of time, we live on the other. In both cases there is a deadline that demands a sense of urgency.

No doubt this woman, who felt greatly indebted to Jesus, gave considerable thought to what she could do to demonstrate her love. As we think about what we can do to show our love for Jesus in these days just before He comes again, we ask ourselves the question, What is of greatest value to Him? And, of course, the answer is, the salvation of other people, and my own. It was for this that He gave His life. The greatest way, then, that we can show our love for Him is by helping others to find salvation.

Exciting Potential

Think of what could happen if every believer—every average Christian man and woman—would put his love into action and do what he is capable of doing to win souls. Think of the transformation it would bring in our own lives, as well as the blessings it would bring to others. What would mean more to a Christian than to hear the words from the lips of Jesus when we meet Him face to face, "You did what you could."

Perhaps it was to bring this kind of encouragement that Jesus left the instruction, Tell it everywhere—the story of a woman, an average person, living in the long ago who loved Jesus very much and who put her love into action with a sense of urgency. She did what she could, and that is all that Heaven requires of us.

Church Planting

Whenever I hear the words, "She did what she could," there passes across the stage of my mind a parade of people who seem deserving of such words of commendation. I think of the church members who decided to plant a new congregation in a flourishing suburb. The area was chosen because of the large number of requests for literature and so on in the interest file from people in that section. A small nucleus from the mother church found a suitable meeting place within this target area where Sabbath services could be conducted. Members from another church assisted in systematically visiting paid-up customers of literature evangelists. Many Bible studies developed from among these names.

Other church members specialized in people whose names came as a result of our radio and television programs. A third group followed up interests from our missionary journals.

Today there is a new congregation in that suburb with a church building of their own. Eighty-nine percent of the new members are converts resulting from systematic follow-up.

When friendship visits revealed an interest, appointments were made for weekly Bible studies. Some who were visiting used the Encounter lessons and the Dukane projector. Others used the gift-Bible method and The Bible Says lessons. No doubt other methods were used also. But the point is that because of the definite plan to plant a new church, and because of systematic follow-up of prospect names, there is a flourishing new congregation in that suburb today. Of those who had a part, certainly the Lord can say, "They did what they could."

Personal Projects

Now I am thinking of a dedicated Christian physician with a busy practice. Every Thursday night he conducted a Bible study in his home and invited interested patients to attend. From this pool of interests flowed a steady stream of persons who were baptized.

Even as I think of this I recall three other physicians who had variations on this plan. One taught a Sabbath school class in his church and invited patients to attend. Among his fruits were the pastor of another denomination and his wife. Another physician opened his home one night a week for a Bible study, but invited a layman to give the study. Another doctor used his large office reception room as a venue for the one-night-a-week Bible study. Each man saw many baptisms resulting from the combination of medical ministry and Bible studies. Of each of these physicians surely the Lord will be able to say, "He did what he could."

Now the scene has changed. On the stage of my memory I see a housewife reading the weekly newspaper. She and her family had been praying each day for the people in their territory. Nothing seemed to happen until this Thursday afternoon when the mother read in the weeky newspaper about an accident. A little boy had been struck by a passing car. He had been rushed to the hospital, where it was discovered that, fortunately, his injuries were not fatal.

The newspaper gave the name of the boy's parents, but it was not familiar to the mother. However, she realized that the accident had happened in her territory. "That family is one of our families!" she exclaimed, and found herself praying, "Lord, bless the Jackson family and especially little Bobby."

Even as she prayed, the Holy Spirit flashed suggestions into her mind: "You've always said you couldn't give Bible studies and that you didn't feel comfortable handing out literature. Here's something you can do. You can go to that home and tell the family that you read of the accident and you're sorry. Ask if there's anything you can do to help. Perhaps the mother needs someone to stay with younger children while she goes to the hospital to visit Bobby. Maybe she needs transportation. You should go."

She went. She was able to minister to human needs and gained new friends in the process. As a beautiful friendship developed and her new friend asked questions, the woman who said she couldn't do it found herself sharing literature and Bible studies. And two people joined the church.

She did what she could, and when she used the abilities she had, God increased her abilities. He will do the same for you and me. "All who put to use the ability which God has given them, will have increased ability to devote to His service."—*Christian Service*, p. 106.

Think what would happen if 50 percent of our lay people would cultivate one friendship contact and have one person to take regularly to the next evangelistic series involving their church. Two out of three of those who attend evangelistic meetings on a regular basis are baptized.

There were 3,850 Seventh-day Adventist churches in the North American Division at the end of 1978. That year 30,422 people were added to church membership. That is an average of eight new members per church. Think what would happen if, in addition to what we are already doing, eight laymen in every one of North America's churches would win just one soul a year. Our baptisms would double. If only four laymen in each church would win a soul each we would see a 50 percent increase in our growth rate. Do you find yourself responding to this challenge, saying, "With God's help I'll be one of those laymen"?

Tell it everywhere, wherever the gospel is preached. Tell about the woman of the long ago, an average person like most of us, who loved the Lord very much. She put her love into action. She did what she could. Think what would happen if every church member in all the world would demonstrate his love for Jesus by doing what he could to win souls.

Prospects

1. Write down the names of the three people you know who are the best prospects for church membership:

_____   _____

_____   _____

2. List the names of the seven non-Adventists with whom you are best acquainted:

_____   _____

_____   _____

_____   _____

_____

3. List the names of the three relatives for whom you have the greatest burden:

_____   _____

_____   _____

4. Put down the names of the three neighbors for whom you have the greatest burden:

_____   _____

_____   _____

_____   _____

5. List the names of the four business or work acquaintances for whom you have the greatest burden:

_____   _____

_____   _____

6. Be sure each of these names is on your prayer list. Ask the Lord to show you what you can do to answer your prayer.

Suggestions for Discussion

1 Discuss the exciting possibilities of each church member doing what he can to show his love for Jesus by having a soul-winning project.

2 Discuss the parallels suggested in this chapter between the woman in Mark 14:8 and Seventh-day Adventist church members today.

3 Under which of the following conditions would you expect the work in your town to grow most rapidly:

a. One church with 1,200 members

b. Two churches with 600 members each

c. Four churches with 300 members

d. Six churches with 200 members

e. Twelve churches with 100 members each
Discuss reasons for your answer.

4 Talk about when and how to plant a new church.

5 One of the best ways to start a successful soul-winning project is to discover people with an existing need that can be met by loving service. What are some such needs that you can think of?

6 Discuss soul-winning projects that are especially suited to members' specific careers.

7 Discuss soul-winning projects in which an entire family can engage.

8 Talk about how our willingness to accept soul-winning responsibility may affect the following:

a. The Holy Spirit's ability to work through us.

b. Our interest in participating in training programs.

c. The attitude of fellow church members.

d. Our own morale.

9 What methods do you think would be best to use to win the three people whose names you placed under No. 1 of the previous page?

WE ARE HIS WITNESSES

There is no portion of Scripture that helps us to capture the spirit of apostolic Christianity more than the book of Acts. And in that book there is no passage more vibrant with this spirit than chapter 5.

In verse 12 of that chapter we read, "And by the hands of the apostles were many signs and wonders wrought among the people."

Signs and wonders are not restricted to apostolic times. Every time a life is transformed by the converting power of Jesus Christ, that is a miracle—a sign and a wonder. Many of you who are reading these words are living miracles, because your life has been completely changed through the power of Jesus Christ.

"Miracles tend to occur along the cutting edge of evangelization. Because the principal purpose of God in doing miracles is to prove His existence and the validity of His gospel, we should expect a greater concentration of miracles when we are attempting to prove the reality of God and the truth of His message than when we are carrying out other activities of the church."—David A. Womack, *The Pyramid Principle of Church Growth,* p. 101.

"The church I see in the future has a high degree of lay participation. The role of the clergy will be to teach laymen how to evangelize their own communities and to create the conditions in which spontaneous evangelistic movements will occur. The role of the laity will be to preach the gospel, present an effective Christian witness in every human setting, and to bring converts into the kingdom of God."—*Ibid.*, p. 133.

Verse 12, of Acts 5 says that the disciples, "were all with one accord." "The phrase 'one accord' appears 13 times in the Bible, 11 of them in the book of Acts.... The basic undergirding of love led them [Christ's followers] to a unity of spirit and they were willing to give all they had—their money, their farms, their possessions, their lives—to get the job done."—Leroy Eims, *The Lost Art of Disciple-Making,* p. 115.

It is when there is unity and harmony among the people of God that we can expect manifestations of God's miracle-working power in signs and wonders. It is when there is unity that God is able to bless His people with growth.

Verse 14 states, "Believers were the more added to the Lord, multitudes both of men and women."

Whenever God's work is prospering as it was in those days, we can expect opposition from the enemy. Verse 17 describes such opposition: "Then the high priest rose up, and all they that were with him, . . . and were filled with indignation." Some Bible margins say, "They were filled with envy."

Their hostility caused them to resort to violence. "They laid their hands on the apostles, and put them in the common prison" (verse 18). These words portray a vivid scene in the ongoing controversy between good and evil.

The angels of heaven, with their miracle-working power, were on the side of the apostles. We must always remember that we also have angelic allies in our warfare with the forces of evil. "All Heaven is in activity, and the angels of God are waiting to cooperate with all who will devise plans whereby souls for whom Christ died may

hear the glad tidings of salvation."—*Christian Service,*
p. 259.

> PRINCIPLE: *Angels cooperate
> with soul winners.*

"The angel of the Lord by night opened the prison
doors, and brought them forth" (verse 19).

Humanly speaking, we might expect the angel to say,
"Look, you're free, you're outside the prison. This is
your opportunity to slip out of town quietly under cover
of darkness." But this was not God's message through
the angel. The angel said, "Go, stand and speak in the
temple to the people all the words of this life" (verse 20).
Notice those bold action words: *go, stand, speak.* The
angel told the apostles to do the very things for which
they had been imprisoned.

The New Life

How much is wrapped up in the expression "All the
words of this life"? The apostles had discovered a new
life in Christ. Their life had begun in the sinfulness that
involved the race, which at best meant 60, 70, or
perhaps 80 years with nothing to look forward to. The
new life was eternal life—one filled with joy and
meaning here and now, and the assurance of an eternity
beyond. It was such a dramatic discovery they couldn't
keep quiet about it. It was the theme of their every
conversation. They had good news to share: A Saviour
has come; repentance is possible; sins can be forgiven.
"We know, because our lives have been changed!" they
exclaimed.

It was their testimony of this new life that gave

144

power to the witness of the apostles. Personal testimonies that are spontaneous, natural, and genuine are no less effective today than they were then.

There are many different kinds of testimony. The one we think of first is of how Christ has changed our lives. Then we may think of testimonies of answered prayer, of the keeping power of God, His providence in relation to faithfulness in tithing or Sabbathkeeping. There are those who have testimonies telling of God's power to heal.

An interchange of personal testimonies is helpful. Some members have stories to tell relative to the Sabbath, tithing, adornment, employment, or marriage. When you recognize that a person you are studying with has a problem in one of these areas, invite a church member with the appropriate testimony to accompany you on the study for three or four weeks before coming to the issue. After your prospect and the church member have become acquainted, the testimony can be shared at the right time.

There is also what I call a church testimony. Let me illustrate by relating the experience of Elsie Collins, a wealthy woman who frequently gave clothes to the Dorcas Society. She worked with the women at the Community Services center for two years before she was baptized as a result of the witness of the women there.

Elsie was already a senior citizen when God led her to the Adventist Church. Soon after her baptism she was traveling to town on the bus when she began to witness to her seatmate. Her face was radiant as she told about the wonderful church she had recently joined. She talked about the sermons that had answered a lifetime's accumulation of questions and of the wonderful sense of security that had come to her now that she belonged to a church family. She spoke of the warmth of church fellowship she enjoyed with brothers and sisters in her

145

new-found faith. With enthusiasm she told of what her church was doing to relieve human suffering and to carry on the ministry of Jesus Christ. So genuinely enthusiastic was she that her seatmate began to ask questions, which is a good sign. Before the two parted, arrangements had been made for Bible studies, which ultimately led to baptism. The testimony of Elsie Collins awakened in another the desire for what she possessed.

The angel that opened the prision door gave instructions to the apostles that said in effect, Continue sharing your testimony. Considering their night in prison, we could certainly understand if they had decided to sleep in the next morning. But the record says, "They entered into the temple early in the morning, and taught." Before the high priest even realized they were no longer in prison, they were teaching the people.

There is a great deal of human interest in verse 23. The officers who had been sent to get the prisoners were extremely reluctant to admit they had escaped. It took them a long time to get to the point.

First, they took time to mention that they found the prison "shut with all safety." That is exactly what one would expect. Prisons are supposed to be shut!

Then they took pains to describe the guards on duty standing in front of the doors. But, finally, they had to admit the problem. There was just one thing wrong— there was nobody inside!

What a picture of suspense and disappointment. What a picture of the frustrations facing those who oppose the work of God. Can't you visualize the expressions on the faces of the chief priests and the high priest when they received this news? Then, at that very moment, to add to their humiliation, a messenger came with the announcement, "Behold, the men whom ye put in prison are standing in the temple, and teaching the people" (verse 25).

146

This time the captain went with the officers and "without violence" brought the apostles before the high priest.

To understand the impact of the next few verses, we need to reread Acts 1:8: "But ye shall receive power, after that the Holy Ghost is come upon you: and ye shall be witnesses unto me both in Jerusalem, and in all Judaea, and in Samaria, and unto the uttermost part of the earth."

The Forgotten Commandment

The apostles saw in these words from their resurrected Lord a reaffirmation of the gospel commission. They recognized a divine command to witness. So when the high priest commanded them not to teach in the name of Jesus, they were confronted with a command of man directly contrary to the command of their Lord. They were caught between God's command to witness and man's command not to witness.

They had already made a good start on this assignment to begin in Jerusalem, because the high priest exclaimed in exasperation, "Ye have filled Jerusalem with your doctrine" (Acts 5:28).

We are first to be systematic in the division of our field. "When the Lord systematically divided the world field into four districts and commanded the disciples to bear the message simultaneously to Jerusalem, Judea, Samaria, and the 'uttermost part of the earth,' He gave us a definite Program by which every lesser field, down to the smallest, is to be systematized for the work of witnessing."—J. E. Conant, *Every-Member Evangelism*, p. 36. This is the Jethro principle of breaking the task into small segments and delegating responsibility.

The early Christians were keenly aware of their individual responsibility. It was this sense of their obligation to obey the command of God that brought them into disfavor with the civil authorities. We are fortunate that we still have freedom to witness in many parts of the earth.

In verse 29, the reference of Peter and his fellow apostles to the conflict between human and divine command is recorded in the terse statement, "We ought to obey God rather than men."

The apostles harbored no uncertainty or misconceptions regarding their identity. They declared emphatically, "We are his witnesses" (verse 32). This is an affirmation we might do well to repeat frequently.

Huss and Jerome were burned at the stake because they could not keep the good news to themselves. They could not remain silent when they had a knowledge of the way to eternal life in Christ. What about you and me? Is it the threat of physical punishment or death that keeps us from witnessing?

Where are Christ's witnesses today? Where are those who are willing to face imprisonment and persecution rather than to neglect His command to witness? The answer from each born-again believer should be, "We are His witnesses!" regardless of the circumstances.

> PRINCIPLE: "We are his witnesses."

It is vitally important that the laity discover and recognize their role as ministers and witnesses. This is the first and basic step. "The first step in the renewal of the church is to encourage as many laymen as possible to see themselves as ministers."—Francis O. Ayres, *The Ministry of the Laity*, p. 20.

Returning to our story in Acts 5, we find that, the

respected Gamaliel was finally able to quiet the angry Sanhedrin with words of wisdom, "If this counsel or this work be of men, it will come to nought: but if it be of God, ye cannot overthrow it" (verses 38, 39).

The apostles were then beaten for no other offense than witnessing in the name of Jesus Christ. Again they were commanded not to speak in His name and then released. They went on their way, not complaining about the hardships they were forced to endure, but rather "rejoicing that they were counted worthy to suffer shame for his name" (verse 41).

As the curtain descends at the close of Acts 5, we catch one more glimpse of a model that should encourage and inspire us: "And daily in the temple, and in every house, they ceased not to teach and preach Jesus Christ" (verse 42).

The apostles were Jesus' witnesses then. We are His witnesses today. The work that God began through them He will finish through us as we demonstrate by our total dedication that we are His witnesses.

Conflict Resolution

Conflict: The commandments of men versus the commandments of God.

God's Commandment

"Go ye into all the world, and preach the gospel to every creature" (Mark 16:15). "Ye shall be witnesses unto me" (Acts 1:8).

Man's Commandment

"Did not we straitly command you that ye should not teach in this name?" (Acts 5:28).

Conviction: "We are his witnesses" (Acts 5:32).

Resolution: "We ought to obey God rather than men" (Acts 5:29).

Suggestions for Discussion

1 Discuss the statement that "miracles tend to occur along the cutting edge of evangelization."

2 Talk about what we can do to create "conditions in which spontaneous evangelistic movements will occur."

3 Why do you think there is such power in personal testimony?

4 Is a lack of unity an excuse for individual inactivity? Did Paul give up trying to win converts in Corinth because of the inconsistencies and even open sin in the lives of some of the members?

5 What are the angels waiting for according to *Christian Service*, page 259?

6 What does the new life in Christ mean to you? Do you have something to share?

7 Discuss various ways we can create an atmosphere in which others will ask us questions about spiritual matters.

8 If you lived in a country where the law forbade speaking to others of Jesus, would it create a problem for you personally? What would you do? What did the early apostles do?

EVERY MEMBER A MINISTER

God is patiently waiting for the individual members of His church to realize their identity as witnesses. Every member is to be a minister. One of Satan's most successful strategies has been to confuse the church on this issue. Well does he know that the finishing of the work depends upon the relationship of the church to this principle. "The work of God in this earth can never be finished until the men and women comprising our church membership rally to the work, and unite their efforts with those of ministers and church officers."— *Gospel Workers*, p. 352.

We have justifiable concern over doctrinal changes that took place during the dark ages of apostasy. But equally as hurtful to the accomplishment of God's purpose were the organizational changes that took place during the same period. Satan will continue to enjoy an advantage in the struggle between good and evil as long as the false concept prevails that only the generals engage in warfare while the men and women in the ranks look on as spectators.

In the apostolic church the only difference between the apostles and the other members of the church was that of office and not of function. When persecution scattered the early believers from Jerusalem, the members, "except the apostles," "went every where preaching the word" (Acts 8:1, 4).

The Priesthood of Believers

The "clergy" might be thought of as that segment of the body of Christ ordained by God and men to function exclusively as ministers. In most cases this group derive their support from the church. In the light of the New Testament, which teaches the priesthood of all believers, the "laity" must also be recognized as ordained by God to function as ministers.

Martin Luther recognized this: "All Christians are truly priests and there is no distinction amongst them except as to office. . . . Everybody who is baptized, may maintain that he has been consecrated as a priest, bishop or pope."—Luther's Manifesto, *To the Christian Nobility.*

Many other scholars share Luther's understanding that in the New Testament the clergy and laity are one in function. "The two words *klèros* (clergy) and *laos* (laity) appear in the New Testament, but, strange to say, they denote the same people, not different people."—W. E. Robinson, *Completing the Reformation: The Doctrine of the Priesthood of All Believers,* p. 17.

Stephen, the first Christian martyr, was a layman. The one who stirred Samaria, the woman whom Jesus met at the well, was a lay person. The one who first introduced Christianity to Africa, the treasurer of Ethiopia, was a layman.

Melanchthon, Calvin, and Moody were laymen. So also was John Bunyan, the author of *Pilgrim's Progress.* Bunyan spent twelve years in jail for lay preaching. Greater even than the misery of his own confinement was his concern for the impoverished condition of his wife and four children, one of whom was blind. But Bunyan said, "I have to preach."

This is the spirit of God's *laos* in every age—men and women who say by their actions, Jesus did so much for me, I must preach. I must knock on doors. I must seek the lost. I must give Bible studies. I must be a witness.

Bishop Lightfoot says, "All Christians are God's laity (*laos*) and all are God's clergy (*klèros*)."—J. B. Lightfoot, *The Christian Ministry*, p. 20.

The term minister in our English Bibles is a translation of the Greek word *diakonos*, which means servant. Jesus came into the world to minister, to be a servant. "The Son of man came not to be ministered unto, but to minister, and to give his life a ransom for many" (Matt. 20:28). Each individual member making up the church body is called to continue the ministry of service which Christ began. Every member is to be a minister.

The Lord's plan to use His gifts to the church "to equip God's people for work in his service" (Eph. 4:11, 12, N.E.B.), is unfortunately obscured by the punctuation of the King James Version. The intent in the original seems clear: apostles, prophets, evangelists, pastors, and teachers are not given their gifts that they alone should minister, but rather that they should equip and train the entire membership to minister. "The main part of the ministry of the clergy should be to enable the laity to fulfill their peculiar, inalienable ministry."—Hendrik Kraemer, *A Theology of the Laity*, p. 167.

Every Church a Training School

The special ministries, such as pastor, evangelist and teacher, are to assist the laity, and not vice versa, as we have usually presumed. This concept of the ministry of the laity in no sense eliminates the need for the offices manned by full-time workers ordained to equip church members for service. If every church is to be a training school there must be a staff qualified to instruct. There must be on-the-job training by which new members are apprenticed to experienced workers. More than theoretical instruction must be provided. Actual practice is a necessity.

Training should be offered in specific areas such as meeting new neighbors, reclaiming inactive members, witnessing to close friends and relatives, winning whole families, reaching the youth, and getting decisions.

Could we expect discerning businessmen to invest heavily in an operation that harnesses only 10 percent of its potential manpower while 90 percent remains idle? Is it pleasing to God when we attempt to use money as a substitute for men? When men give themselves in service they will also be willing to give their money in sacrifice.

In the apostolic church sacrifice was a normal way of life. This was true also of the early days of the Advent Movement. In both cases there was a great degree of lay involvement. So it will be again. When church members become involved in service and we experience the momentum of a movement, their dedication will inspire dedication in others. Enthusiasm is contagious. Unity and participation produce a willingness to sacrifice.

There is the potential for tremendous inspiration when the entire world is divided so that every Seventh-day Adventist family is praying for the people living in the specific geographical area assigned to them. As the conviction that he is to be a minister grows stronger for the individual church member, he will add to his ministry of prayer other forms of ministry for the people in his territory. When he commits his energies and talents to the task, his finances follow. This was demonstrated in the total dedication of the early church members, and it will be repeated in this end-time.

God has left it with His church to devise ways and means so that the gospel of present truth may reach all men everywhere. The logical place to begin is with the names in the interest file. Ways need to be found to win these people.

Churches and companies around the world are responding to this challenge. Seventh-day Adventists in Tanzania, inspired by the practice of the early Christians, have developed their own distinctive greetings. One of the greetings exchanged by early Christians was "Maranatha"—the Lord is coming. Some of our African members are greeting each other with such words as "What are you doing in your territory?" Indonesian believers are challenging each other with the greeting, "Rumah ke rumah"—house to house. In the Philippines, "Bahai, bahai," conveys the same message.

The people of God are beginning to respond to the challenge to carry the Word of God to every man's door. God revealed that this would take place. "In visions of the night, representations passed before me of a great reformatory movement among God's people. . . . Hundreds and thousands were seen visiting families and opening before them the word of God."—*Testimonies,* vol. 9, p. 126.

At Cape Kennedy, in Florida, manned spacecraft were launched on journeys to the moon. Similarly, each local church should be a launching site from which members are sent out for Christ in their locations whatever their vocations. Every Christian is called to be a missionary wherever he is stationed in life. Your pulpit may be your station on the assembly line, your work bench at the factory, a desk at the office, or a seat beside a fellow passenger on a train, bus, or airplane.

Holy Spirit Power

God is waiting for us to take seriously the gospel commission. When we do, the promised power of the

Holy Spirit will be given to us. "The Holy Spirit will come to all who are begging for the bread of life to give to their neighbors."—*Christian Service*, p. 252.

We cannot do this work in our own strength. It is "not by might, nor by power, but by my spirit, saith the Lord of hosts" (Zech. 4:6) that the work will be finished. Yet we must ever remember that the Spirit of the Lord operates through consecrated human instruments to finish the work. We must never lose sight of the fact that every member is a minister.

Suggestions for Discussion

1 What can be done to help members see themselves as ministers? Does terminology have a bearing on this?

2 In the statement quoted from *Gospel Workers*, page 352, where does the initiative that will unite members and leaders for a finished work seem to originate?

3 What can we do to change the circumstances that delay the finishing of the work?

4 List areas of specific training you feel are needed in addition to those suggested in this chapter.

5 Do you agree with the premise that increased spirituality, activity, efficiency, and effectiveness will result in increased giving?

6 Discuss opportunities for witness related to your employment.

7 What should be our primary motive in all Christian service?

8 Numerous inspired statements tell us that the Holy Spirit will provide miracle-working power for finishing the work when the majority of God's people become involved in soul-winning outreach. Such involvement cannot be forced. What can lay leaders, and laymen in general, do toward reaching majority involvement?

APPENDIX I

Results of Neglecting Follow-up

Delay in follow-up can be critical. It is true in the service of the King of the universe that "the king's business required haste" (1 Sam. 21:8).

A man and two women called at the home of an It Is Written viewer as they were following up names from the interest file. When at the door they announced the purpose of their visit to the woman of the house, she said, "It took you so long to come. You are too late, but come in anyway."

"It was my daughter who requested a visit," she explained. "She watched It Is Written faithfully for many months. One Sunday morning three years ago, at the close of a telecast, she told her father and me that she had made up her mind to join the Seventh-day Adventist Church. We invited our pastor over in an attempt to dissuade her, but her mind was made up. She said she was not being fed in our church.

"Our daughter wrote and asked It Is written to send a representative.* Every week she expected a visit, but months passed and no one came. One day some people called from another religious group. They talked to our girl and tried to interest her in their beliefs, but she told them that she had decided to become an Adventist.

---

* All the It Is Written names are forwarded to the nearest pastor to be followed up by him or by lay persons.

"Two weeks later these people came back. They said their doctrines were similar to the Adventists'. They were very persistent, and by that time our daughter was disappointed that no Adventist had come in response to her request. So she agreed to study with them. She joined their organization and is now a very active member.

"If she had to leave our church, my husband and I would have been much happier for her to join your church than the group she did join. But you are three years too late."

APPENDIX II

Table I

There was no consistent pattern to the accession rate of the Pleasantville church. It was up one year and down the next.

ACCESSION
RATE

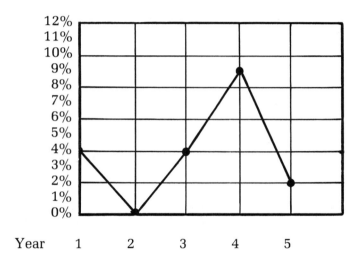

Note in Table II, line 1, that the Pleasantville church membership was recorded for each of the five preceding years, using the membership figure as it was at the beginning of each year. On line 2 additions to membership through baptism and profession of fatih were recorded. This is the accession rate. This information was placed in the appropriate column for each of the five years. In order to show total membership growth some churches prefer to add an additional line on which they list additions to membership by transfer. To show net growth it is necessary to subtract those lost to membership by death, apostasy/missing, and those transferring out by letter. The Pleasantville church chose to consider only the accession rate, that is, additions by baptism and profession of faith, so lines 3 to 6 are blank.

Line seven shows the percentage of growth in accessions for the Pleasantville church. This was found by dividing the number of additions through baptism and profession of faith for the year by the church membership figure at the beginning of that year. For example, for the first year under consideration the membership was 50. During the year there were two additions by baptism or profession of faith. The two divided by 50 gave an accession rate of 4 percent. On line 8 is recorded how many Adventists were required to win one new member. This was discovered by dividing the membership figure at the beginning of the year by the number of converts added during the year. In this case it was a matter of dividing 50 by 2, which shows that it required 25 members to win one new member during the year.

With this picture before them of what the immediate past history of their church looked like, the Pleasantville church members turned their thoughts to the future. They decided how they wanted the church growth pattern to look for the next five years.

The average accession rate for the five-year period under survey was approximately 4 percent per year. It fluctuated from zero percent to almost 10 percent in individual years.

Table II
Where We Came From

Five-year history of the Pleasantville church.

Years ago	Five	Four	Three	Two	One	Now
Membership at beginning of year	50	52	52	54	59	60
Additions by baptism and profession of faith	2	0	2	5	1	
Additions by transfer of letter						
Losses by transfer of letter						
Losses by death						
Losses by apostasy/ missing						
Percentage of growth	.04	0	.038	.092	.016	
Adventists required to win one member	25	- -	26	11	59	

NOTE: To show net growth, it is necessary to subtract from total additions those lost to membership by death, apostasy/missing, and those transferring out by letter.

To simplify, we have rounded off decimals to the nearest whole number except in the case of percentage of growth.

Table III
Where Are We Going?

Pleasantville's five-year goal for growth.

The church board voted to aim at an accession rate of 6 percent for the first year in their five-year projection and to increase this by 1 percent each year so that by the fifth year they would reach a 10 percent accession rate.

Year	One	Two	Three	Four	Five	Six
Membership at beginning of year	60	64	68	73	80	88
Additions by baptism and profession of faith	4	4	5	7	8	
Additions by transfer of letter						
Losses by transfer of letter						
Losses by death						
Losses by apostasy/ missing						
Percentage of growth	.06	.07	.08	.09	.10	
Adventists required to win one member	15	15	14	10	10	

Table IV

What Actually Happened at Pleasantville.

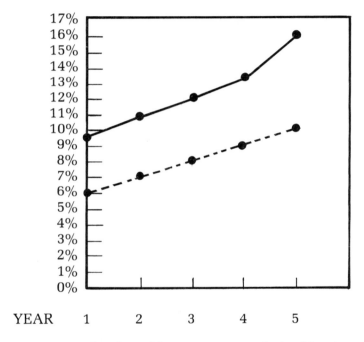

ACCESSION
RATE

YEAR 1 2 3 4 5

NOTE: The dotted line represents their objectives for accessions, and the solid line represents their actual growth by accessions.

How to Take a Community Religious Survey

The first question in the Community Religious Survey, "Is there a God?" is one that anyone can answer without a moment's hesitation. It serves well to get people into the survey. There are two questions to probe possible interest in Bible study, and the question "In your opinion, how does one become a Christian?" reveals something of the person's understanding of the plan of salvation.

The survey can be taken by one person or, for training purposes, by a team of two or three. At the door, we smile and say, "Hello, we're conducting a Community Religious Survey, and we'd appreciate it if you'd take just a moment to give us your opinion on these questions that you can answer with Yes, No, or No Opinion. In your opinion, is there a God? If you say Yes, I'll put a check mark here. If you say No, I'll put a check mark here, and if you say No Opinion, I'll mark it here."

This simple introduction to the survey immediately sets the person at ease. In your first sentence, you tell him why you're there. Next, you explain that he is free to say Yes, or No, or No Opinion. Most people relax and become very friendly during the survey. In urban areas where security may be a problem, the survey can be taken at the door. In rural areas, it usually will be easy to get an invitation inside by simply suggesting, "You don't mind if we step in for just a moment, do you?"

Those conducting the survey should be neatly dressed and, aside from a woman carrying a handbag, should have nothing more than a clipboard with survey blanks attached. These forms may be duplicated on either 8½-by-11 or 5½-by-8½ paper. The reverse side may be used for recording the name and address plus any other information that will help to make future visits more meaningful. These forms provide an excellent way of preserving a record of the spiritual condition of each person in your territory.

As soon as you are out of view, and while the information is still fresh in your mind, you will want to record any pertinent information such as the names of little children in the family so that you can call them by name on your next visit. You will also want to keep a record of materials you left, such as a Bible study lesson. If people say they are not interested in religion, accept this without argument, but make a note for your next visit so that you can try a health or temperance approach.

Transition From Survey to Bible-reading Guides

It is not difficult to make a transition from the survey to the offer of Bible-reading guides. It can be done like this: "Thank you for taking the time to give us your opinion on these questions. We appreciate it very much. And now, just before we leave, here's something I think you may be interested in." As you hand the person the first lesson of a Bible course, say, "These reading guides are basically lists of questions that you and I and everybody wonders about. There aren't any answers given but it tells you where you may look in your own Bible to find them. Thousands around the world are using these reading guides and benefiting from them. I thought you would like to know about them too. Parents tell us that they are really a help in answering their children's questions about God and the Bible. If you feel this is something that would be of benefit to you and your family, they are free, and we will be happy to leave the first one with you today and keep you supplied with new ones each week. If we leave more than one or two, there is a tendency for them to pile up and become a burden, like the laundry and the ironing, so we leave just one or two at a time."

Some surveyors find it effective to say, "I'm doing these too, and perhaps we can plan to get together once a week and compare our answers." The weekly visits then naturally develop into Bible studies simply by reviewing the questions and answers. Those who have access to audio-visual Bible study equipment might want to supplement the studies with the help of these very effective tools.

Once the person has accepted a Bible-reading guide, you have a reason for returning each week. These weekly visits provide an opportunity to build friendships.

It is after an individual has accepted a reading guide that I introduce myself. The tension of the early moments of the visit has now worn away and it is much easier to concentrate on names. I do it like this: "By the way, I guess I didn't introduce myself. My name is ————, and with me is ———— ————. Now, I should write down your name so that I remember to come by next week with your next reading guide. Your address here is . . ." Hesitate and they will give you the address. It is often wise to write down their phone number, especially if they live at a distance and you want to determine whether or not they are home before making your return visit.

During subsequent visits, it is good to watch for opportunities to take along something that lets the person know you want to be his friend. This can be something you've made or something out of the garden. It could be a birthday card for one of the children. Any of these things say, "I want to be your friend." This is vitally important, because we must establish a relationship of friendship with the prospect before we can win him for the Lord. We win friends, not strangers, and one of the purposes of the Community Religious Survey is to make friends.

Rarely will people ask why you are conducting the survey. But if they do, give an honest and forthright answer. We are doing it because we have been instructed, "Wherever a church is established, all the members should engage actively in missionary work. They should visit every family in the neighborhood, and know their spiritual condition."—*Christian Service*, p. 12. I try to translate this into language meaningful to the person I am visiting. I say something like this when they raise a question: "We are from the Adventist Church, and, as you may know, our church offers several services to the community such as Five-Day Plans to help people stop smoking, nutrition classes, and Bible courses. We have a concern for the physical and spiritual well-being of our community, and we feel we need to become acquainted with the thinking of people who live here." You may frame the answer in your own words.

Occasionally you may meet this question, "What church are you from?" With a smile I reply, "We are from the Seventh-day Adventist Church. Do you have any friends or relatives who are Adventists?" Asking a question keeps the questioner's mind occupied and sometimes his answer will give you additional information. Personally, I do not mention my church affiliation at the beginning of my visit unless asked, and I rarely am.* However, near the close of every cordial visit, I casually mention, "You said your church background is _____. We are from the Adventist Church. Do you have any friends or relatives who are Adventists?"

We have been kind to the people. We have taken an interest in the things they are interested in. We have not

---

* One exception to this is in rare cases where we are being mistaken for members of other groups against which there is strong prejudice. In such neighborhoods I begin, "We're from the Adventist Church and we're taking a Community Religious Survey."

argued with them, and even in those cases where we have not been able to leave a Bible lesson, we have at least made a good public relations visit for the Lord and His church by thus identifying ourselves. I like to carry Bible correspondence enrollment cards and perhaps radio-TV logs in my pocket to leave at the door when no one is home, or with those who choose not to accept the Bible reading guide.

COMMUNITY RELIGIOUS SURVEY

	Yes	No	No Opinion
1. In your opinion, is there a God?	☐	☐	☐
2. Is there life after death?	☐	☐	☐
3. Is Christ coming again?	☐	☐	☐

4. Who is Jesus, according to your understanding?

    ( ) Son of God
    ( ) Saviour of man
    ( ) Creator
    ( ) Prophet
    ( ) Not sure

5. Do you feel you understand the
Bible as well as you would like? ☐   ☐   ☐

6. What church did your
parents attend?_____

7. Do you belong to the
same church?_____

8. About how often are you able
to attend?
Weekly____ Monthly____ Seldom____ Never____

9. In your opinion how does one become a Christian?

_____

_____

10. If you had the opportunity,
would you like to study the Bible more?

        ☐   ☐